A Matter of Style: Women in the Fashion Industry

By Linda Leuzzi

Women Then — Women Now

FRANKLIN WATTS
A Division of Grolier Publishing
London   Hong Kong   Sydney
Danbury, Connecticut

For my mother, Palma De Clara, and my aunts,
all hardworking women of fashion who sewed and
beaded the dresses that American women wore.
Thanks for your conscientious, persistent work ethic.
And for your sense of fun.

L. L.

Interior design and Pagination by Carole Desnoes
Photographs ©: Archie Lieberman: 105; Burdines: 141; Corbis-Bettmann:
11, 15, 19, 20, 29, 30, 33, 57; Gamma-Liaison: 71 (Allen), 73 (Benali), 67
(Jeff Christensen), 77 (John Chiasson); Linda Leuzzi: 128, 136; Lord &
Taylor Archives: 55; Lowell Historical Society: 25; Marbeth: 130; The
Metropolitan Museum of Art Costume Institute: 52; Sam Ogden
Photography: 112, 116; Talbots: 108; Travis Huchison: 122; UPI/Corbis-
Bettmann: 37, 50, 60.
All other photos are courtesy of subjects.
Author photograph ©: Kim Rienzi

Library of Congress Cataloging-in-Publication Data

Leuzzi, Linda
    A Matter of Style: Women in the Fashion Industry / by Linda Leuzzi
        p. cm.—(Women then—women now)
    Includes bibliographical references and index.
    Summary: Explores the important role women have played in the
growth and development of the fashion industry and includes interviews
with women working in the varied fashion industry of today.
    ISBN 0-531-11303-5 (lib.bdg.)   ISBN 0-531-15831-4 (pbk.)
    1. Fashion—United States—History. 2. Clothing trade—United
States—History. 3. Women—United States—Interviews. [1. Fashion—
History. 2. Clothing trade—History. 3. Women—Interviews.] I. Title.
II. Series.
TT504.4.L48 1996
338.4'774692'092273—dc20   96-33960
                                                            CIP
                                                            AC

Contents

Author's Note

Fashion and the methods used to create it are centuries old. The eyed needle, for example, which is still in use today, has been found in the remains of Stone Age settlements. The scarf, an important fashion accessory, was originally used as a tied bag to carry objects. In the fourteenth century, scarves decorated the upper body from shoulder to hip and were tied at the waist. By the seventeenth century, scarves were wrapped over a woman's head and shoulders.

Not surprisingly, women have been involved in the design, creation, and promotion of fashion over the centuries. This is especially true of American women, who have been passionate, persistent, and resourceful in their efforts to develop fashion—as they were helping to shape a country. Their important contributions continue today.

The first part of this book, Women Then, chronicles how American women helped develop fashion in times past, from the early inhabitants of the continent to women of recent decades. It looks at how American women made cloth and clothing, at their influence in the labor force as mill and garment workers, at their shaping of fashion trends, and at their achievements as businesswomen, inventors, and designers.

Women Now provides a current overview of the fashion industry and a description of some of the roles women play in creating fashion—the jobs they fill as garments move from idea to finished product on a clothing-store rack. Interviews with fourteen successful women in American fashion provide a firsthand look into this fascinating world. This group of women includes a designer and company president, a buyer, a pattern maker, a co-owner of a clothing store, a booker, a model, a textile fashion director, a collections manager in a major museum, a fashion director of a women's magazine, and a vice president and general merchandising manager.

Following the women of earlier decades, these women have persevered in the visions that they saw for fashion and for themselves. It was an honor for me to interview them and to hear their stories.

L. L.

Part One

Women
Then

The Beginnings of the Fashion Industry

The American Influence

In the late 1850s, Ellen Demorest, known as Nell to her family, carefully laid out two dozen patterns in her Philadelphia living room so that women customers could touch them and see for themselves how the sleeves, collar, skirt, and other parts of a garment looked on paper forms. Demorest had been a successful milliner and now her new venture was selling patterns of women's and children's clothing, in specific sizes. Nell, with help from her sister, Kate Curtis, was eager to explain how the thin paper patterns would enable a sewer to transform a piece of cloth into a fashionable, well-fitted dress. Both women had apprenticed in traditional dressmaking for seven years. Along the way, they had developed a more precise dress-cutting system and their children's dress charts had won two medals for their accuracy in 1853 in an international exhibit at the Crystal Palace, a huge hall referred to as the Temple of National Industry.

Nell and Kate were taking risks in this new venture. Would women really be interested in trying these patterns? Some advance publicity had been sent out for the opening day, and Demorest was gambling on a hunch. Clothing patterns weren't new, but a sewing machine that could be used in the home had just been invented, and Nell reasoned that the time was right to offer sized paper patterns that were inexpensive, uncomplicated to use, current with fashion details, and compatible with the new sewing machine. She wanted to make them available to women all over the country.[1] It was a first because patterns hadn't been mass marketed before.

If Demorest was nervous, reassurance came quickly. A large crowd of women dressed in the bell-shaped skirts of the day had gathered outside the front door, down the stairs, and well along the sidewalk, waiting to enter and eager to see her new patterns in specific sizes.

By 1875, Nell Demorest's business had distributed 3 million paper patterns internationally. A working mother with four children, she was building a business empire. She traveled overseas to report on the fashion world and ran a huge fashion emporium on East Fourteenth Street in New York City that sold her patterns as well as custom-made clothing. Among her diverse ventures were also a cosmetics business and a tea business that she had specifically established for poor women, to enable them to earn commissions.

The key marketing vehicle for the patterns was a fashion quarterly launched by her husband, William Demorest. *Mme. Demorest's Mirror of Fashions* first appeared in 1860, with advertisements for the patterns and a free sample attached. Popular even during the Civil War, when it reached a national circulation of 60,000, the fashion quarterly eventually became a monthly.[2] The magazine staff included American designers who developed the fashions illustrated in each issue, and Nell's sister Kate, who adapted French designs to more sedate American tastes.

The saleswomen in the emporium showrooms were well paid and fairly treated; they included African-

Mme. Demorest's Mirror of Fashions

American women, who received the same wages as other workers and were encouraged to attend company functions. Nell Demorest also quietly crusaded for women's rights, and backed the formation of the first women's club.[3]

From Clothing to Fashion

Although Nell Demorest was an important creative force in her time, the role American women played in developing fashion didn't begin with her or even with the women of the colonial period. The stage had been set centuries before. The concept of paper patterns had been around since the Middle Ages, when European tailors used them as measuring guides to cut cloth.[4] During this period, society began to become stratified; social classes based on differences in wealth and position began to appear. The different groups wanted their clothing to reflect their status. They wanted to wear clothing that would set them apart. That's when fashion began to emerge.

The western part of the world is generally credited with being the area in which tailors and dressmakers produced most of their work, and medieval Europe is where the momentum began.[5] Historical records show that some women were employed to work as tailors outside the home around this time. Tax rolls of 1379 and 1380 from two particular towns in England—Oxford and West Redding—list several women as seamstresses and shapesters, another term for tailor.[6] Women also made silk and thread; they were working industriously at this craft in Florence, Italy; Paris, France; and London, England.

Women were also beginning to establish their own guilds.[7] Paris had exclusively female silk- and thread-makers' guilds in the fourteenth century. Female guilds in the textile and clothing trades existed in other French towns, as well as in villages and cities in Germany, Italy, England, the Netherlands, and Belgium from the fourteenth to the seventeenth centuries.[8] And by the beginning of the fifteenth century, the production of women's clothing was basically a female domain.[9]

Guilds had first appeared in the twelfth and thirteenth centuries in Europe, as informal groups of both women and men who worked at the same craft in the same area of a town or village. At first, the guilds used their power as a group to organize feast-day processions in honor of the patron saint of their craft, or they collected money for a guild member who was ill or experiencing difficult times. They became much more influential in the fourteenth and fifteenth centuries, especially the merchant guilds that lobbied their local rulers and won control of trading rights. With these rights, they were able to acquire wealth and establish a power base against any competition.[10]

In time, these guilds regulated training in their craft, who could be admitted to the craft, the hours in their workday, quality standards, and prices. In predominently male guilds, wives or daughters of craftsmen could be admitted. But some male guilds admitted women on their own merit.[11]

Important changes appeared in the developing industrial landscape. Local village production began to shift to specialized regional production, with the goods sold for long-distance trade. New technologies undermined the painstaking artisanal work of the craft guilds. As male workers felt threatened economically, they protected themselves by excluding women and enforcing guild laws. In Lyon, France, a silk guild known as the Fabrique de Lyon, founded in 1545, restricted women from working as loom operators, an occupation that received better pay.[12] Even in the all-female guilds, women were still restricted from making the most lucrative products. For example, in London, women silk weavers, no matter how skilled, could produce only piecework. Male silk weavers had the exclusive right to make the whole cloth. This privilege was sanctioned by the guild's rights that the men had won from their rulers.[13]

Couturiers and Haute Couture

Two developments helped women make significant gains in the fashion world. In 1675, French seamstresses, angry that only master tailors had the right to create women's dresses, brought their own petition to the throne. They sought and won the privilege of designing women's dresses—previously reserved exclusively for men.[14] After a three-year apprenticeship in cutting and dressmaking, women could open their own businesses as couturiers, or seamstresses.[15] Gradually, rulers of neighboring countries followed France's lead, and granted the right to design dresses to women. Later, the term *haute couture*, which means "high sewing" in French, would be used for the work of designers who prepared new fashions each season.[16]

About a hundred years later, a woman named Rose Bertin, a dressmaker, designer, and style adviser to the French queen Marie Antoinette, introduced what we call couture, or custom-made, design.[17] Bertin was also a milliner and sold bonnets, fans, frills, and lace to clients including members of royal families from Paris, London, Madrid, and St. Petersburg. Because the shape of women's dresses was basically the same from year to year, milliners were in demand for the creative ways they could arrange accessories and make clothing look different and unique, and Bertin was skilled at this. Bertin visited the French queen and her court twice a week, listened to their requests, made suggestions, and then created new looks. Showing a flair for marketing, Bertin had her new styles recreated in miniature, as garments for dolls, then sent the dolls to courts throughout Europe. These dolls became enduring fashion staples that traveled across continents; colonial women in America relied on them for the latest European styles.

The Art of Homemade Clothing

Native Americans had already been living in North America for 20,000 years when the first European settlers arrived in the fifteenth and sixteenth centuries. The

In an old woodcut, women discuss the latest styles—as presented on fashion dolls

North American Indian groups the settlers encountered were using weaving techniques in making their clothing.[18] After the arrival of Spanish settlers, weaving workshops were set up in some of the Pueblo Christian missions in the valley of the Rio Grande. The cloth produced was so prized by the Spaniards that it served as a form of tax payment; thirty-three inches of cloth had to be provided by each family as a tax payment to the Spaniards. To escape Spanish rule, some of the Pueblo Indians fled to the Navajo region in the late seventeenth century. There, they taught the Navajo women some of their special weaving techniques. Some other Native American clothing makers were honored within their groups. Among the

Plains Indians, the Lakota bead and quill specialists were prominent.

The European settlers moved into a land with trees that grew down to the water's edge, and with rocky areas, sand hills, and swamps. In the early days, they concentrated on survival. Colonial women worked along with men at what historians call "household manufactures," producing items they needed to survive in this wild, new place. Among their responsibilities was the making of clothing.[19]

What did making clothing involve? Many garments were made from flax, a crop that was planted in May and then processed through a number of stages to make linen. Flax is a plant with a tough core and outer layer, and it takes perseverance to extract its fibers. The stalks were cut at the roots at the end of June or July and laid out to dry. Then they were combed with an iron wire comb, and bundled and stacked. The stacks were then piled under running water so the leaves would rot. After five days, the leaves were removed. The fibers were separated yet again by a heavy instrument.

The next step involved the spinning wheel, a common fixture in the early American household. With it, family-grown flax could be spun into fine linen thread. A low wheel propelled by a foot pedal enabled women to spin the flax. They could rock a baby and tend to other chores while spinning. After making the thread, there was yet another process before the thread could be woven into cloth. The women soaked the thread in hot water, then in ashes, and then in clear water, as a method of bleaching.[20] The final product could then be woven into garments, towels, tablecloths, and other everyday goods.

Wool, from the coats sheared from sheep, was made in a separate process, which yielded a thread that could be knitted into stockings and mittens or woven into cloth. Wool was simpler to prepare than flax, but a different type of wheel was used to spin wool, and the process involved a lot of walking back and forth. A woman might walk a total of twelve miles in an ordinary day of spinning.[21] Sometimes wool and linen were combined; wool provided warmth and linen, strength.

Colonial families were sometimes large, and a woman might need to spin and make clothes for ten children, herself, and her husband. The states of Massachusetts and Connecticut recognized the importance of spinning in a law enacted in 1640, which stated that every family had to spin a specific amount of flax each year or they would be fined.[22] But spinning was not always solely labor—spinning competitions and matches became a common form of entertainment.

Because of the colonists' way of life, clothing was basically plain and functional. Homespun material was much more durable and economical than material that could be purchased. In the pre-Revolutionary period, making cloth also served as a political statement, as the colonists tried to avoid buying imported goods to protest taxes and import restrictions imposed by the British Parliament. Colonial women banded together and agreed to boycott British goods, rejecting imported tea for their own herbal teas, and wearing only clothing that they could spin or weave themselves.[23]

Clothing that Won the War

Not much has been written about colonial women's contributions to the Revolutionary War effort, but it was significant. Wives of soldiers provided many of the army's support services, such as cooking, washing clothes, and nursing. Some became spies and couriers, and a few even fought. They also contributed clothing—clothing that provided protection and kept the troops warm. When the war began, and army supplies were scarce, a call was sent out for 13,000 warm coats for the Continental army, to be ready in time for a winter assault against the British.

Colonial women filled the order. These warm, homemade coats were prized. Families of soldiers killed at Bunker Hill were given payments so that their coats could be passed on to other soldiers.[24]

Late in the war, a national women's organization that became known as the Ladies Association raised money for the troops by going from house to house asking for contributions. A group of New Jersey women collected the substantial sum of $15,500. The women wanted a guarantee that the money collected would be directed specifically for the troops' needs, but General George Washington had other thoughts and there was a tug-of-war by letter over the money. Washington finally suggested that the women use the money to make shirts for the soldiers. Linen was in short supply, but the women completed more than 2,000 shirts in three months, and these were handed over to the deputy quartermaster general in Philadelphia in December of 1780. Each creator inscribed her name in the shirt as a sign of support.[25]

After the Revolutionary War, the preference for homemade clothing continued. Importing clothing and fabrics meant relying on other countries, and Americans had fought so hard to be free that independence and self-sufficiency were valued in all areas of life. In 1791, Alexander Hamilton wrote that four-fifths of the American people, in some areas, made all their clothing at home.[26] Also, to protect the newly developing American textile manufacturers, Congress instituted a tax on imported cloth, including cotton, wool, and linen.[27]

In addition to making the thread and cloth, colonial women also worked at dying the cloth. They created colors for designs for their cloth by boiling blossoms, leaves, roots, berries, and bark. The colors that they created were surprisingly vibrant. From the indigo plant, they produced shades of blue. Red hues came from the madder root, or from ground-up cochineal insects. The colonial women experimented to develop recipes to make their

An antique French fashion doll, used to show the new styles of the period

dyes: hickory bark would produce a greenish yellow color when mixed with some alum, and walnut dye became more intense when a solution containing copper was added.

However, not everyone wore homespun, home-dyed clothing. Fashion did exist in the colonies, and Boston and New York were the major fashion cities. "Babies," descendents of Rose Bertin's dolls, were little mannequins dressed in the latest dresses, hats, coats, and accessories brought over from England and Europe. Their miniature garments were copied by milliners and dressmakers in major towns and cities.[28] Luxurious fabrics were imported from Europe by prosperous merchants of the North and South.[29]

Milliners were important people. Demand for their skills had begun in the Middle Ages, when Milan was the main source for fashion and accessories. The term *milliner*—a merchant who sold hats—evolved from the Italian word *Milaners*.[30]

Hats were as significant as women's dresses; besides being an accessory, they shaded the face from the sun and

An early dressmaking establishment

kept the head warm in the blustery months. Although hat styles were said to have changed seventeen times between 1784 and 1786,[31] most women couldn't afford the luxury of a new hat every year. A good milliner could make the latest hat, or she could also revive the previous year's version, using ribbons, flowers, and feathers to completely change its look.

In the young United States, retail millinery shops began to appear. These were small local shops, usually run by the owner—most often a woman—who dealt directly with the customer. Wholesale milliners emerged on a large scale by the mid-nineteenth century, making enough hats to supply shops and department stores.[32]

Nell Demorest's career path provides a good example of how these retail and wholesale millinery enterprises developed. In 1843, at age eighteen, Demorest started her own millinery business, with an assistant, in her hometown of Saratoga, in upstate New York. It was a good location because Saratoga was a prosperous resort town that in the summer attracted a wealthy crowd of stylish women. Ambitious and creative, Demorest relocated to Troy, New York, a year later. Troy was a leading millinery center then and Demorest eventually found a job as a supervisor for a millinery wholesaler with merchandising markets in New York and Philadelphia.[33] Wholesale milliners employed women in local small towns to work on hats in their own homes, and it was one of the last businesses to transfer from the home to factory.[34]

Singing the Union Song

"Some of us took part in a political campaign for the first time in 1840, when William H. Harrison, the first Whig president was elected," wrote mill worker Harriet Hanson Robinson. "We went to the political meetings, sat in the gallery, heard the speeches against Van Buren and helped sing the campaign song."[1]

Working in the Mills

Robinson was a Lowell, Massachusetts, mill worker. She had grown up in Lowell, where her mother ran one of the town boardinghouses. At the time, in the early part of the nineteenth century, many single women, mostly daughters of farm families, were leaving their homes to find work in New England mill towns—weaving, spinning, warping, and carding wool and cotton. Robinson's autobiography, *Loom and Spindle*, provides a look at what life was like for women as textile workers, along with a glimpse of their thoughts, hopes, and dreams. These workers saw their employment as a way to escape the drudgery of the farm and a way to gain what they considered independence. By 1816, two out of three industrial workers were women, and the mill town women were recognized as an important labor force through the 1840s.[2]

The town of Lowell was named for Francis Cabot Lowell, a wealthy businessman who perfected the power loom used in English factories. The power loom offered a new technology. It played a major part in the Industrial Revolution, changing textile production from what was basically a home industry into a mass production industry.[3]

Textile production involves two steps: spinning, in which fibers are stretched and twisted into yarn or thread; and weaving, in which a piece of fabric is constructed by connecting groups of threads or yarns at right angles to each other. In many colonial homes, both steps were completed. A child might participate in hand carding, to align woolen fibers. A mother might spin on a wool wheel to make the yarn, and a father might work a loom, which was a rather large piece of equipment. Some women spun for wages; spinning 1,600 threads was considered a good day's work.[4] There were also craftswomen who produced weaving for more affluent families. In the early part of the nineteenth century, some even went from town to town, carrying along fabric pattern books, staying with families, and weaving for them.[5]

By the nineteenth century, immigrants were streaming out to the American frontier. They needed sturdy cloth for their clothing, and Frances Lowell was able to supply it through mass production. He set up an efficient factory system—The Boston Manufacturing Company—in Waltham, Massachusetts, in 1813, and his looms were powered by a ten-foot waterfall on the Charles River. He needed intelligent, dexterous employees to work these machines, and he found a ready supply for his labor force from among the local New England women. By setting up a supervised environment with boardinghouse residences, he offered these women respectable positions and a chance to make their own money.[6]

After Lowell died, two manufacturing entrepreneurs purchased a new site—with bigger expansion opportunities than there were in Waltham—in Pawtucket Falls, where the Merrimack River crashes through rocky rapids. The site even had a canal that could be converted to a power canal to generate electricity for the mills. Work began on the new mill town in 1822. It was completed a year later and named Lowell.[7]

Lowell, Massachusetts, where Harriet Robinson worked, at one time had 33 mills and 500 boardinghouses.[8] Not all the employees were women, but most were. Lowell women received about half what men received in pay. Their average day was twelve to fourteen hours long, and they worked in conditions that were often poor; windows were kept closed, even on the hottest days, because it was better for the fibers.[9] But in the early years of the mill, Robinson recorded that even though the day was long, the women weren't overworked and there were breaks and rest periods.[10]

Historically, this was the first sizable group of women to live away from home and, for many of them, it was their first exposure to a range of thoughts and ideas.[11] In 1834, of Lowell's 6,000 workers, almost 5,000 were women between the ages of seventeen and thirty-four.[12] Although the paternalistic mill owners carefully supervised large portions of their workers' lives, they also provided access to lectures, literary clubs, language classes, and all the books their employees could read after work.[13] The women were free from housework and could concentrate on their work; at the end of the day, a dinner was ready for them at the boardinghouse. Robinson wrote about coworkers who were aware of the outside world and interested in current political issues. They attended night classes and wrote for their own newspaper. And they were

The Merrimack mills and boardinghouses
in Lowell, Massachusetts

taught certain skills; Robinson referred to it as manual training.

There was no doubt that the mill owners reaped many benefits from this arrangement. But the women were not totally passive and pliable. In February 1834, a mill worker was fired after arguing with a company agent at a meeting about planned wage cuts. Word of her firing spread and 800 women from the Lowell mills got up from their work stations and marched through the town.[14] Ten years later, Lowell mill worker Sarah Bagley formed the

Lowell Female Labor Reform Association when she learned that the Massachusetts legislature was organizing a committee to consider a ten-hour day. The reform association members collected 2,500 signatures and some of them testified before the committee in support of the bill, although the proposal wasn't passed.[15]

Working conditions were good for about the first twenty years, then the continuous wage cuts, increased work loads, long days, and crowded housing became outrageously exploitive.

Harvesting Cotton

By 1848, the town's mill workers were churning out 50,000 miles of cotton cloth a year.[16] Cotton cloth had been known since the sixteenth century in Genoa, Italy. It was initially woven for domestic items, like pillow covers, and then lingerie. By the late eighteenth century, the cloth was used in women's dresses,[17] and its production leaped after the cotton gin's invention by Eli Whitney in 1793.

Whitney, a skilled, Yale-educated mechanic hired by plantation owner Katherine Greene, was urged to develop an efficient machine to separate seeds from the cotton. Some stories claim that Whitney wouldn't have gotten a patent without Greene's help. Supposedly, he became stuck on a technical problem. The cotton clogged the wooden teeth of the machine he constructed. Greene suggested using wire as a kind of comb, which worked.[18]

Whitney persevered and got the patent. But the cotton gin needed the raw material—cotton—to process, and the cotton didn't just magically appear. Someone had to do the hard work of harvesting it in the fields. In another part of the country, a large female labor force was doing that work—the enslaved blacks of the American South.

Slave women worked in the cotton and woolen mills in the South under white supervisors. And they also picked cotton. On the plantations, they worked in the fields. They went up and down rows of cotton plants, dragging bags behind them, picking 150 to 200 pounds a day under a hot sun for fourteen hours.[19] Then it was time for chores, cooking, making clothing, tending gardens. One son recalled that his mother worked as a cotton picker and as the head spinner. She returned from picking cotton perhaps a couple of hours early to prepare supper; then supervised the other women after the meal.[20] Unfortunately, as slaves were kept illiterate by law, there aren't many written accounts of their lives.

Some blacks escaped this life. Marie Therese Coincoin, a Louisiana slave born around 1742, lived with a Frenchman who bought her freedom and gave her a major landholding. A smart, enterprising woman, Coincoin ran a profitable plantation that raised cotton as well as other crops, and bought her children's and grandchildren's freedom. Coincoin's 13,000-acre plantation and buildings are now a national landmark.[21] In the North, free African-American women worked as dressmakers, weavers, and spinners.

Social and Fashion Progress

In the pre–Civil War period, women were taking large steps forward in American society and in the young fashion industry. Mary Kies, who developed a straw-weaving process that was used in hat making, became the first American woman to receive a patent in 1809.[22] Oberlin College in Ohio, founded in 1833, became the first college to admit women along with men to its campus. During the 1840s, American women began traveling out West on their own. Several hundred graduates from Catherine Beecher's Hartford, Connecticut, teaching academy took long, bumpy trips on railroads, boats, and stagecoaches to reach remote towns and western villages in order to establish schools.[23] By mid-century, Sojourner

Truth and Frances Harper, both powerful African-American lecturers, were riveting audiences in the North with their antislavery speeches[24] and Elizabeth Taylor Greenfield was the first African-American concert singer to give a command performance before royalty, when she performed before Queen Victoria of Great Britain.[25] In 1861, Matthew Vassar endowed the first all-women's college in Poughkeepsie, New York. Astronomer Maria Mitchell, the first women to join the Academy of Arts and Sciences, was on its faculty.[26]

Changes were affecting the fashion world as well. New York City had become a major commercial center. The new steamships easily maneuvered the Hudson River, bringing in more merchants with all kinds of fashion wares. Wide streets such as Fifth Avenue and Broadway, pleasant for walking, were also good locations for retail stores. By the 1860s, an amazing number of women were putting up signs on the major avenues and side streets announcing their millinery and dressmaking businesses. Mrs. C. Donovan, a busy dressmaker, opened a shop on Fifth Avenue and Mme. Harris & Sons, an exclusive millinery house that charged anywhere from $25 to $100 for a hat,[27] appeared on Waverly Street and Broadway.

An Individual Style

Europeans were still the fashion trendsetters, but as American women moved into many new areas, they began pressing for individualism in their clothing. Steamship travel helped bring in the new looks, by way of wealthy travelers who returned from trips abroad with the latest accessories and clothing.[28] But European fashions weren't merely slavishly copied. For one thing, the heavy wool material of a lovely English outfit would be too warm for southern women; also a style that might have been considered divine in the Paris court, would have been too fussy for an American event. *Godey's Ladies Book*, a magazine introduced by Louis Godey in 1837, described the latest fashions, and even showed them. The illustrations were drawings reproduced through a technique using steel-engraved plates and were known as fashion plates.

Imagine having to wear long skirts while planting a garden, mounting a horse, or climbing stairs. If you didn't grab your skirts or bend in a certain way, you would trip, topple over, or expose something that shouldn't be seen. It was a confining way to live. By mid-century, some

A fashion plate from *Godey's Ladies Book* for July 1875

women were ready for something acceptable to wear that gave them more freedom. Amelia Bloomer, editor of a feminist newspaper, promoted such an outfit in 1850. Bloomer admired an acquaintance's ensemble of a sashed tunic worn over balloon-type pants and showed the look in her paper.[29] While this new fashion wasn't chosen for every woman's closet, a fair number of women did wear it. It was called the freedom dress.

The freedom dress drew enough attention to provoke a New York State legislator. He spoke out against it, and so did the newspapers.[30] The style lasted only about three years, but it did plant the idea that clothing could be comfortable, and women who enjoyed sports adapted versions of the outfit for swimming and calisthenics. Surgeon Mary Walker initiated her own manner of freedom dressing. Walker wore pants when her work took her to the Civil War battlefields. Fortunately, male legislators were smart enough to overlook her costume and concentrate instead on her medical skills and service contributions when they awarded her the Congressional Medal of Honor. She was the first woman to receive it.[31]

Ready-to-Wear

By the end of the eighteenth century, a middle class had begun to emerge. Instead of making their clothes, some of the more prosperous people were able to afford to buy them. Dressmakers and tailors began offering a small selection of ready-made clothing in their shops. Ready-to-wear women's clothing, which could then be altered to fit, became increasingly available.

The caption with this nineteenth-century illustration stated that it represented Amelia Bloomer wearing the revolutionary new outfit she promoted.

The War of 1812 is generally credited with the first surge of mass-produced, ready-to-wear garments, although clothing for sailors in the busy port of New York was actually the first ready-to-wear clothing offered.[32] Three to four hundred seamstresses reportedly worked for the United States Army Clothing Establishment. Tailors began accumulating a large inventory of apparel; one Boston tailor advertised an inventory of 5,000 to 10,000 items of male clothing.[33]

Mass producing men's and boy's clothing was fairly easy; the styles didn't change that much and the clothing was standard. But women's clothing was another matter. The intricate trims and details of earlier nineteenth-century styles were too hard to duplicate on a large-scale basis, so dressmakers and home sewers were kept busy producing these fashions. Then, about the 1850s, methods of making specific items such as shawls, loose wraps, and capes in large quantities were developed, and mass production for women's clothing began.[34] Ready-made women's suits became available in 1868, at prices ranging from $25 to $250.[35]

While war creates devastation and death, it has often created new opportunities for business. About 2,600,000 soldiers, from the North and the South, fought in the Civil War, between 1861 to 1865. The enormous need for uniforms, and the availability of the sewing machine—which had been introduced in the States in the 1840s by Elias Howe—helped ready-made garments become a reality on a large-scale basis. Further, as the men were off fighting battles, business operators began to tap an alternative large workforce, and one that was willing to accept lower wages. Women in the North and South were running businesses and plantations, which they had done historically while their husbands or fathers were off fighting; now they also filled their places in factories and plants. After the war ended, many stayed in these jobs because of a mate's death or disability.[36]

In an 1879 woodcut, women work on the manufacture of garments in a New York City workroom.

The growing number of middle-class American women who now rolled up their sleeves to work in business and to play sports wanted distinctive clothing. There were now machines that made lace and covered buttons. Details such as tucking and embroidery were easy to produce with the new technology. And more women could now afford to wear bright colors, formerly an expensive choice, because of new, less costly analine dyes—synthetic dyes made from chemicals.[37]

Department stores evolved from the old dry-goods stores, where household products and fabric, trims, buttons, and other items for the making of clothing could be purchased. In New York, for example, dry-goods stores started springing up in lower Manhattan, close to the dock area where ships and merchandise were constantly coming in. Not surprisingly, the city's first department stores began appearing in the surrounding streets in the 1820s. Over the years, they grew in size and changed location. Merchant A. T. Stewart caused a sensation when, after a series of smaller stores, he opened a huge store in 1862. It took up an entire city block on Broadway, was five stories high, and had two basements. His store carried ready-to-wear and custom-made clothing. An 1875 illustration of a workroom at A. T. Stewart shows rows of women assembled at tables sewing garments for the store's customers. In general, most department stores had such workrooms.[38] The people employed there often were part of the growing stream of immigrants who were coming to this country, seeking the safety and opportunity that America offered. Many of them settled in New York and were hired for work in the production of textiles and clothing.

Fashion Invention

By the last quarter of the nineteenth century, new technology and inventions had led to unprecedented changes. In transportation, railroads were carrying people across the country and streetcars were taking city dwellers to work. Homes were lit by electricity instead of gaslight or candlepower. Women were responsible for some of the new technologies. By 1877, more than 2,000 women held government or patent inventions.[39] These women, who had proved the uniqueness of their inventions through detailed presentations and intricate drawings and models, created a variety of innovative products and techniques. Amanda Theodosia Jones from Boston patented a canning process in 1873 and started a business that laid the groundwork for the pure food industry.[40] And

Margaret Knight of Springfield, Massachusetts, made a fortune from an 1870 patent for a machine that produced square-bottom brown paper bags.[41]

A number of the patents from this period concerned clothing items. Olivia Flynt, a Boston dressmaker who felt that the women's corsets of the time were inhumane, patented the Flynt Waist in 1876. Corsets had been stiff forms, with laces from beneath the breasts down through the waist area. When the laces were pulled together tightly, the corset pushed in the waist, making it look smaller. It was uncomfortable and confining. Flynt set out to improve the undergarment after she saw how painful the corset was for a customer. Flynt's product was made of flexible, breathable material and it supported the breasts and smoothed the body, something corsets didn't do. It was popular for at least two decades.[42]

By the end of the century, more than 5 million women were industry wage earners.[43] Women were also becoming inventors and businesswomen, and they had entered professions, becoming doctors, nurses, teachers, lawyers, architects, and scientists. They walked for exercise and played croquet and skated. Their clothes reflected the new freedom in their lives. Separates like the shirtwaist (a blouse), worn with a skirt or with a tailored suit, became the standard fashion for both working and wealthy women. The shirtwaist and skirt could be worn to work, to college classes, and to leisure outings. It was a crisp, neat look that signaled competence. For winter sports, a much shorter skirt was worn, with pants underneath that were tucked into boots.[44]

The Garment Makers

The workforce, including both women and men, had increased tremendously. Immigrants were pouring into the country in record numbers. Seventy-six million people populated the country in 1900 and a third of them were newly arrived immigrants. In 1906 alone, 1,100,735 immigrants arrived.[45] These people were mostly of southern and eastern European Jewish and Catholic origins. By 1910, more than 40 percent of the immigrant population had settled in New York City and the New England cities of Fall River and Lowell. Thirty to forty percent located in Boston, Chicago, Milwaukee, Detroit, San Francisco, and seven other major cities. Twenty percent aimed for seventeen cities that included Seattle and Portland on the West Coast.[46]

The cities held two attractions for the immigrants: opportunities for work and already established ethnic neighborhoods. The newcomers would be steered toward jobs and lodging. And while learning a new language, they could hear the familiar speech of their home country.

Between 1880 and 1910, about 2 million eastern European Jews came to this country. As they settled in and found work, they came to form the largest ethnic group working in the garment industry, which was centered in New York City.[47] Many of the immigrants had already worked as tailors and seamstresses in their homeland, so it was natural for them to gravitate to jobs in the same trade here. The work was hard and the days were long, but there was a chance to accumulate some money to start a storefront business and some were able to do that. But for most, especially those with large families, the challenge was to survive. A typical workweek was sixty hours or longer. The $6 or $7 salary that a male garment worker might average in a week, was cut in half for his just-as-skilled female coworker.[48]

American clothing was considered the highest quality and was the best-selling in the world by the early 1900s. But the workers did not benefit from this achievement.[49] Unfortunately, most wealthy industrialists treated their workers as disposable items. When the employees demonstrated or organized strikes against unfair wages and working conditions, these bosses were powerful enough—

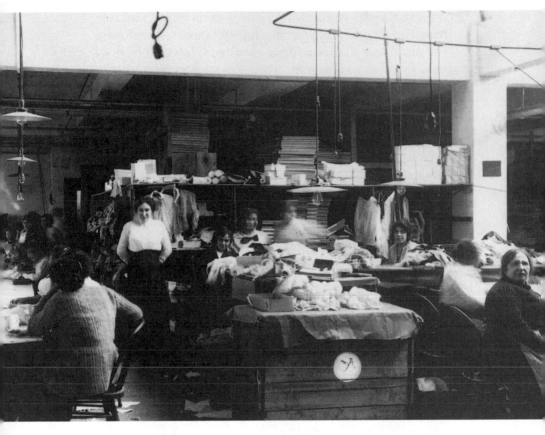

A New York City sweatshop, photographed about 1913

through lobbying efforts, bribes, and personal friend-
ships—to persuade senators, members of congress, and
governors to intercede in their favor. Some of the strikers who fought back lost their lives. Jay Gould, a famous
Wall Street speculator, once said, "I can hire one half of
the working class to kill the other half." This callous attitude wasn't held just by wealthy industrialists; it trickled
down also to other business owners around the turn of

the century. A tremendous labor force was available because of the immigrant influx; thus many employers felt that if one worker refused a company's wages or policies, there was always another, hungrier person to take that place.

The Labor Movement

By this time, American women were becoming part of the labor union movement. They represented 20 percent of all manufacturing workers[50] and, because their pay traditionally was lower, they had already been fighting for their rights for decades. The Knights of Labor, a national labor organization founded in 1869, offered the women their first hope for affiliation with a major union. Membership was open to workers, skilled or unskilled, and that included women—whether they worked at home or in a factory. The organization supported an eight-hour day and the abolishment of child labor. Another goal was the initiation of a cooperative system, where a large part of the economy would be controlled by the workers instead of the industrialists. In their heyday, the Knights of Labor claimed 700,000 members. About 65,000 women were members by 1887, some in the 270 "ladies locals" that were chartered by the Knights. But the organization, unfocused in its goals and activities, lost membership and disappeared by the end of the century.[51]

In 1886, the American Federation of Labor was formed, a national association of trade unions that represented only skilled workers. Their goal was to get as much as possible for the worker through collective bargaining. The AFL had a dedicated president, Samuel Gompers, who led the organization for thirty-eight years. A good number of skilled women worked in AFL crafts; but they were not welcomed as members because they were women. The general attitude was that they belonged at home.[52]

When the American Federation of Labor excluded women from their ranks, women formed their own organizations. The Illinois Women's Alliance was among the more successful ones. A partnership of women's trade unions and middle-class women reformers, the alliance took up a number of issues between 1888 and 1894, including sweatshop regulation, ending child labor, and stopping police abuse of women strikers.[53] The Women's Trade Union League (WTUL)—whose members included working-class women, second- and third-generation college women, as well as prominent society women sympathetic to the working-class struggle—was another. Founded in 1903, the WTUL was the most effective group to form an alliance between lower-, middle-, and upper-class women. One of its main goals was to organize working women and integrate them into the trade union movement.[54] The WTUL was to play a large part in helping women garment workers organize effectively in New York.

Clara Lemlich, an eighteen-year-old immigrant who had fled the violent anti-Jewish persecution in her native Russia, helped to form Local 25 of the International Ladies' Garment Workers' Union (ILGWU), which was founded in 1900. The fiery Lemlich, who sewed shirtwaists, participated in many strikes and was arrested seventeen times.

In 1909, when several thousand women gathered at the Cooper Union meeting hall in New York to discuss a general strike, Lemlich stood up and led the call. The young woman was still sore from a beating suffered at a picket line; it wasn't uncommon for employers to hire thugs to intimidate strikers and some of the police called in to maintain order were just as rough. "I am a working girl," she said clearly and passionately, speaking in Yiddish, "one of those who are on strike against intolerable conditions. I am tired of listening to speakers who talk in general terms. What we are here for is to decide whether we shall or shall not strike. I offer a resolution that a general strike be declared—now."[55]

Lemlich's words reached the sense of unfairness and anger that fellow workers were experiencing and reflected their yearnings. The meeting led to a strike known as the "Uprising of the Thirty Thousand," the largest labor action of working women at that time.[56] As word spread, over the next few days, strikers filed out of their workplaces by the thousands. They poured into twenty strike halls at different places in the city. These strike halls were safe havens organized by the WTUL, where the women could meet to develop strike support, plan picketing schedules, and find comfort from police brutality.[56]

What were the conditions these women were protesting? Wages were first on the list. Besides paying the women lower wages than men, employers could change the wages at will. They could begin with a weekly wage, and then change this policy to piecework wages, or paying workers by the number of pieces, such as a sleeve or collar, that they produced. If the worker did well and produced large quantities of piecework, the following week the employer often lowered the price paid for each piece. Working conditions were a second issue. The factories were called "sweatshops," they were crowded, noisy, stifling, and dangerous. Two years after Lemlich's strike, a tragedy at the Triangle Shirtwaist Factory exposed the inhumane and gruesome conditions in these sweatshops.

The Triangle Shirtwaist Factory was located on the eighth, ninth, and tenth floors of the Asch Building in New York City. The space inside was a firetrap; sewing machines crowded up against each other, dripping oil and piles of cloth were everywhere, and the doors were locked—not only to discourage union agents from entering and organizing the employees, but also to prevent theft and to keep workers from using the bathrooms. When a fire broke out, in 1911, there was no way out. One hundred forty-six workers died, most of them women, because the managers had refused to provide basic safety measures of unlocked doors and fire escapes. Employees were faced with a wall of fire and many jumped from the windows. It was the worst industrial accident in New York's history.[57]

It took events such as the "Uprising of the Thirty Thousand" and the tragedy of the Triangle Shirtwaist Factory to force change. The public was outraged and a state commission was formed to study the conditions that led to the fire as well as what workers were experiencing in the workplace. As a result, strict regulations were eventually passed which included fire safety and factory inspection laws.[58] Because of the efforts of Lemlich, the WTUL, and other women garment workers, and the forceful way they pressed their issues, the ILGWU became a major labor union that is still vital today.

Designing Women

In December 1912, the *New York Times* announced a fashion-design contest, offering cash prizes for best evening dress, afternoon dress, and hat. Ethel Traphagen, a designer for several custom shops, won the evening dress division. Ruth Turner Wilson and Irma Campbell won first and second prize respectively for their versions of an afternoon dress. Wilson went on to become well known as a writer and illustrator of costume history, and Campbell became an in-house designer for Lord and Taylor, a fashionable New York department store.[1]

It was one of the first times that American women designers had been given major attention. A year before the competition, Saks & Company, another well-known New York department store, advertised its in-house American fashions as "our own individual ideas."[2] The word "design" wasn't even used.

Talented—But Anonymous

There were, as the fashion contest proved, American women designers at work. They were creating clothing, deciding what a dress or outfit should look like, if it should hug the body like a column or if it should be full and voluminous, and what decorative details, buttons, lace trim, silver or gold braiding would make it stand out. They were choosing fabrics, looking at the textures and colors, and at how they draped when used. Many dressmakers, too, were acting as designers, producing distinctive garments as they worked along with a customer's specific requests. Elsie de Wolfe, a successful and famous interior designer, asked her New York dressmaker, Mrs. Osborn, to make an outfit with the skirt hem raised six inches above the ground. "I'm tired of sweeping the streets," she said. "I'm dressed in a practical manner, one which the world, if it were sensible, would copy."[3] Wearing her new "walking suit," as she called it, de Wolfe went to Paris and caused a sensation.

American designers became well known for the quality of their ready-to-wear clothing. However, Paris was still considered the place where design trends were set. A Paris-made outfit was a kind of elite uniform. Paris labels were even sewed into the New York-made clothing of import custom houses, shops that offered imported dresses that could be bought as is or adapted. This label misrepresentation was aimed at making the garments more marketable. "American women have been brainwashed into thinking French clothes are superior," claimed the head of one of the shops that used these false labels.[4]

The French Legacy

Why was Paris such a leader? Paris had been thought of as the source of luxurious, elegant garments since the reign of Louis XIV, in the mid-seventeenth century. Known as the Sun King, this ruler felt that sumptuous clothing symbolized the wealth and prestige of his court, and his garments were embroidered in gold and silver and lined in ermine, an expensive fur. Brocade could be worn only by the king, princes in his family, and those he deemed worthy by law, and he gave his courtiers beautiful cloth as gifts. French weavers produced intricate and beautiful silks, gold cloths, velvets, and other fabrics, and Louis also brought in hundreds of lace workers from Belgium and Italy. Because of the king's interest in style and clothing, thousands of Paris tailors, dressmakers, and milliners were kept busy creating new fashions for his court in nearby Versailles, as well as for wealthy Parisians and foreign visitors.[5] By 1712, Paris was so caught up in a fashion fever that a foreigner commented that a suit made forty days earlier was already considered out-of-style by the wealthy.[6]

The Sun King's grandson, Louis XVI, continued this emphasis on luxurious, beautiful clothing. His wife, Marie Antoinette, preferred the title of Queen of Fashion to Queen of France. The French Revolution of 1789 and the overthrow of the monarchy were mere interruptions to the French position of leadership of the fashion scene. Even during this tremendous upheaval, fashion was still a part of Parisian life; fashion magazines reappeared in 1797.[7] So, while the young American nation was still in the process of establishing itself and developing its own style, the expert clothing makers of Paris were already in place, with a strong background of resources, traditions, and skills.

Paris continued to be the fashion center through the nineteenth century. Charles Frederick Worth, an Englishman who began his career in the drapery department of a London department store, moved to Paris with the hope of making his fortune. He set up his own Paris dress salon in 1858 and is credited with starting the haute couture industry. At his House of Worth salon, he designed fashion collections in advance and used models who resembled his clients rather than an idealized woman. These were unique ideas for the time. Worth considered himself an artist and he was; he chose beautiful fabrics including delicately colored silk damasks and silk satins, and he used exquisite details such as crystal embroidery for his gowns.

Another factor that contributed to Paris's position as

a fashion leader was the city's welcoming attitude toward creative people in many fields—painters, poets, writers, musicians, and performers. People eager to explore new directions in fashion, or to work in a stimulating atmosphere with the leading established designers, were drawn to the Paris scene. And, working amid such a concentration of artists, designers would come to call upon some of the famous painters of the era to fashion textiles. In the early years of the twentieth century, a leading Paris designer, Paul Poiret, hired the artist Raoul Dufy. Dufy's joyful, brightly colored paintings of sporting scenes were adapted to textiles. Shortly after, French artist and designer Sonia Delaunay also began producing textile designs, using her signature style, vivid colors, and bold geometrics.[8]

Ethel Traphagen, the 1911 *New York Times* first-prize evening dress winner, also drew inspiration from a painter, American James Whistler.[9] Whistler, who trained in Paris and then lived in London, was influenced by the work of the French Impressionists and by Japanese woodblock prints. He used mysterious, smoky colors in the nighttime scenes of his "Nocturne" paintings,[10] and Traphagen, stimulated by one of these scenes, kept this image in mind when she designed a dress of blue chiffon layered over putty-colored silk. While talented women like Traphagen were designing beautiful, innovative styles, it would be nearly two more decades before America's women designers would begin to be recognized as a force.

Social Changes

After its long domination of fashion, several factors and world events weakened both the preeminence of Paris and America's reliance on Parisian designs. In 1914, Germany declared war on France and many designers such as Paul Poiret closed their businesses and enlisted. With the war raging, Paris wasn't as accessible as it had been. Although fashion did continue to exist in Paris throughout its duration and many of the closed design houses reopened during the war,[11] American store buyers could not flock to Paris as they had. They began to turn to American originals.[12]

On April 6, 1917, the United States joined the war effort. About 15,000 women became part of the Women's Land Army, a farm labor group, and thousands more worked in Europe, in clerical and communications jobs for the army.[13] Women signed up as nurses, ambulance drivers, and volunteers, and it was the first time American women had their own distinctive uniforms.[14]

After World War I, women worked to become a politically powerful group through the efforts of the suffragettes and actively pressed the president's office for the vote. The National American Woman Suffrage Association had steadily built up membership in the preceeding years through a series of efforts, including countless meetings, canvassing, lobbying, fundraising, and demonstrations. Groups picketed the White House for six months, beginning in 1917. By 1919, the Nineteenth Amendment to the United States Constitution was passed, and on August 26, 1920, women were granted the right to vote.[15]

By 1920, women represented 43.7 percent of the total college population; in actual numbers that meant 431,000 women were enrolled.[16] Women were now making significant inroads into areas where they had not been permitted before. In 1921, three African-American women earned their Ph.D. degrees: Eva Beatrice Dykes received a Ph.D. in English from Radcliffe; Sadie Tanner Mossell Alexander earned her degree from the University of Pennsylvania where she was the first black person to receive a Ph.D. in economics; and Georgianna R. Simpson was awarded her Ph.D. in German by the University of Chicago.[17]

Encouraged by the supportive philosophy of the women's colleges and the changing attitudes at institutions that had begun to admit both male and female students, the women graduates saw that many choices were now available to them. The women's institutions in particular fostered a belief that the women could strive to change things for the better, and they did. They combined family *and* reform efforts and influenced major areas of American life, such as labor conditions and politics. A good number chose careers in social work; in this period, women made up two-thirds of the country's social and welfare workers.

Along with these possibilities, other career fields attracted women, and fashion was one of them. Women were hired as fashion editors to write for magazines such as *Vogue* and *Harper's Bazaar*. Others were employed as buyers and sent to Paris, and still others became copywriters who created fashion ads.[18]

American Designers

Elizabeth Hawes, a Vassar graduate, worked her way into a career as a fashion designer and became a well-known fashion industry figure in the 1930s. Hawes had grown up in a fairly prosperous household. Her mother employed a family dressmaker, and the children of the family were involved with decorative crafts, including beading. As a girl, Hawes was given a Paris gown by her grandmother every year and her mother took her on trips to New York City, where they window-shopped, looked for fabric remnants, and visited museums.[19]

As a new college graduate, Hawes sailed to Paris in 1925 to learn about fashion. She carried $300 and her grandmother's diamond ring for funds.[20] She joined the city's vibrant cultural life, living at various times above the Shakespeare and Company bookstore, a place where many of the creative figures of the period, such as writer Ernest Hemingway and composer George Gershwin, came to borrow books or meet. The three-dimensional mobiles that her friend the artist Alexander Calder created provided a reference point for the way she wanted her clothing to move. And the imaginative squiggles and arrows that Spanish artist Joan Miró used in his paintings would later be imprinted on Hawes's capes and vests.[21]

The aspiring designer's first important job was working for a copy house called Doret. Her assignment was literally to steal designs from leading couturiers. She attended their fall and spring shows, making mental notes as the models walked out one by one, and then dashed back to the copy house to reconstruct them on paper. If she was lucky, and a show was so hectic that no one would be likely to notice, Hawes would slip into a quiet corner of the fitting room and copy the designs as models paraded before buyers.[22] Hawes wasn't thrilled with her role—she wanted to create her own designs, not steal someone else's—but the job gave her an insider's view of how the fashion industry functioned.

Hawes learned first-hand the procedures of a couture house. First, the designer, who in most cases named the fashion house for herself or himself, expressed an idea either through a sketch or verbally to a head assistant, referred to as a première. The première interpreted the design and made a cloth version that was draped on a model. This was brought to the designer for approval. After some scrutiny and adjustments by the designer, seamstresses would make a pattern and then cut and assemble the garment.[23]

As an observer, Hawes felt that something was out of balance. The seamstresses, who basically did most of the work, got paid the least while the designer received most of the income. Rejecting this traditional arrangement, she resolved to do things differently when she had her own firm. Later, when she had established her own company and the depression was making survival difficult for everyone, Hawes would ask her women employees (who were often supporting unemployed families) what they needed to live on and paid them accordingly. Sometimes she charged customers what they could afford.[24]

Hawes's second important job was working with designer Nicole Groult, the younger sister of couturier Paul Poiret. Hawes assisted Groult with all the details of putting together a collection—choosing fabric, sketching designs, reworking the garment—and the job gave her the chance to work as a couturier herself. Hawes's time in Paris was valuable. It exposed her to another culture and another way of looking at life. She learned about style by having to determine what was good enough to copy; from Dorset, she learned about the many aspects of running a business; and with Groult, she got to work as an actual designer.

In September 1928, Hawes returned to the United States. She was eager to produce more avant-garde fashions, garments that were unique and experimental. She felt that designers here were not introducing designs that were truly new. Her return coincided with significant changes in the American economic situation that had an impact on all areas of business activity, including the fashion industry. America was beginning to enter the Great Depression, with a stock market crash in 1929 that resulted in many lost fortunes.

As the depression settled in, many rich women who had been accustomed to buying expensive Paris clothing found that they either couldn't, or didn't wish to, continue doing this. An average couture dress in the 1920s might have cost $400, with an added U.S. tariff for clothes imported into the country.[25] There were old money families who were still financially secure, but most tended to be conservative about new fashions. They would buy an expensive, but classic, garment and wear it for several years. At the same time, American manufacturers and retailers were cutting back on purchasing Paris imports to copy because they were so expensive.[26] These conditions helped open the way for American designers.

In late 1928, Hawes set up Hawes-Harden in New York City, with her wealthy cousin Rosemary Harden as backer. The company became Hawes, Inc., two years later

Elizabeth Hawes, described as a "well-known American modiste," was photographed returning to the United States after a 1931 trip to Paris.

when Harden pulled out amicably. It took Hawes four years to assemble a good staff—première, fitter, drapers, and finisher—and every garment was an exclusive.[27] Her designs were extremely popular. After years of the chemise and its straight, boyish silhouette, Hawes showed a return to a more fitted, feminine look. She created clothing for the natural body; her models didn't wear corsets or bras. Hawes's designs were distinct; her trademarks were comfortable, bias-cut clothing that hugged the body, with deep armholes and pockets, and natural shoulders. She used the highest quality natural fabrics for her designs and guaranteed her work.[28] What's more, the average dress cost $195[29]—a price that was a large sum of money at the time, but much less than her comfortable customers were accustomed to paying for their Paris couture garments.

Besides the wealthy, Hawes's clientele included Broadway actresses.[30] Hawes was often photographed in her creation, a pair of suspender slacks (a forerunner of the jumpsuit), worn with soft, flat-heeled shoes. She was irreverent, relaxed, and funny, and she knew how to use publicity to her advantage.

There were other successful designers at the time, including Hattie Carnegie. Probably the most successful American couture designer of the 1920s, Carnegie's clothes would, in the 1940s, be selected and worn by the Duchess of Windsor.[31] But Hawes was one of the most important designers in the 1930s, as well as the first visible American designer.[32]

What did a Hawes dress look like? The Costume Institute at the Metropolitan Museum of Art in New York City houses about 70,000 articles of clothing. Included in its inventory is an evening dress designed by Elizabeth Hawes about 1935. The garment is a short-sleeved, surplice gown made of a softly colored woven silk, with pale gray, royal blue, and brick red stripes. A thin stripe of green shot with a subdued metallic thread also runs

An Elizabeth Hawes dress, preserved at the Costume
Institute at the Metropolitan Museum of Art

through the fabric. There is a matching custom-made silk-crepe slip in the dominant pale gray color. The dress is slightly high-waisted, with small, meticulously sewn flat pleats under the breasts; the skirt has two-tiers, with a slight train. The effect is slender and graceful, and while it doesn't look intricate, it is. Hawes designed the dress so that the straight grain of the fabric joins perfectly with the stripe. The V-necked back is secured by twenty-five covered buttons that match the stripes on which they rest. The seams are finished, not cut.[33]

Other women were beginning to gain attention as fashion designers. They included Nettie Rosenstein, the daughter of immigrants, who started out sewing for clients in her home; Muriel King, who dressed some of Hollywood's emerging stars such as Katherine Hepburn and Ginger Rogers; and Claire McCardell, who became known for her coordinated sportswear.

Emerging from Anonymity

How were these designers promoted? As fashion editor of *New Yorker* magazine, Lois Long began mentioning home-bred talent in the mid-1920s.[34] Publicist Eleanor Lambert championed American designers in the press releases and photos she sent to newspapers nationwide in the late 1930s, making it easy for editors to run a fashion story by providing the names and descriptions of the styles in her copy. Lambert took over the best-dressed list, originally started by a group of Paris couturiers in the 1930s, and in the 1940s was influential in the founding of the Metropolitan Museum of Art's Costume Institute.[35]

Probably the biggest step forward in introducing these designers to the public was initiated by Dorothy Shaver, Lord & Taylor's vice president at the time, who would go on to become the country's first female president of a major retail store. Lord & Taylor had been a popular New

York department store since its beginnings in the early nineteenth century, but it had never featured American designers by name in its displays. In 1932 Shaver began promoting American designers in advertisements, and their names were featured in window and interior displays.[36] A Lord & Taylor press release stated that Shaver promoted more than sixty American designers in an eight-year period. Many were women, including Elizabeth Hawes and Muriel King who were featured in Shaver's first group of American designers.[37]

Movies were becoming a major fashion influence. Edith Head, who was hired to sketch fashion designs in the 1920s for Paramount Studios, was in charge of the entire design department fifteen years later. At Paramount and at Universal Studios, where she later worked, Head designed for 987 Hollywood films. Her designs included beautiful hand-beaded dresses for Carole Lombard, who starred in 1930s and 1940s films. Head once commented that women stood in line to see what actress Joan Crawford was wearing. Eventually, Head won eight Oscars for her work.

Wartime Style

The outbreak of World War II in September 1939 meant—as in the World War I period—that the United States was cut off from the Paris fashion scene. While the German occupation of the city of Paris didn't eliminate French couture completely, American fashion designers and buyers were, for the most part, unable to see the new lines. This gave a strong fashion push to homefront designers.[38]

America's war effort lasted from 1941 to 1945. With men signing up for combat and other military duty, 6 million women joined the workforce.[39] For the first time, women were thrust into roles that had been available to men only. The poster image of "Rosie the Riveter," a no-

A photograph from the 1940s of Dorothy Shaver, the first woman president of major retail fashion store

nonsense woman in overalls with rolled-up sleeves displaying a muscled forearm, symbolized these American working women. They wore coveralls and slacks for industrial jobs such as wiring boards for aircraft companies and cutting out aircraft parts with drill presses.[40]

For the first time, women were also able to enlist in the armed forces and 350,000 signed up for the various service branches, including the Women's Army Corps and the Women's Airforce Service Pilots.[41] Jackie Cochran flew a plane called a B-26 for the Women's Airforce Service Pilots, an aircraft men initially didn't want to fly because they considered it unsafe; subsequently 150 women flew B-26s.[42] Uniforms created by designers were offered as an enticement to sign up for the armed forces and volunteer services. Designers Liz Hawes and Claire McCardell created uniforms; Hawes planned one for the Red Cross Volunteers and McCardell's contribution was for the Red Cross Motor Corps.[43]

Besides pushing American women to the labor forefront, World War II also affected how women dressed. A regulation known as L-85, announced in 1943, virtually froze clothing styles because any major change would require extra labor, and the government had first call on the nation's laborforce. Factories that had been churning out the latest fashions were now making uniforms. Wool was used for uniforms; silk was sewed into parachutes, gunpowder sacks, survival sacks, and scarves for the pilots. Cotton cloth was fashioned into summer uniforms and sandbags.[44] Since material was a valuable commodity needed for the war effort, there were standard measurements for dresses, suit jackets, and pants, as well as for coats and blouses.[45] Beadwork or rhinestone buttons might accessorize a dress, but mostly, the 1940s silhouette was a narrow look with broad shoulders. It was also sleek, tailored, and professional, and it promoted the image of strength; women were shouldering the burden of the nation's production.

Women working in factories during
World War II adopted coveralls as their uniforms.

Postwar Style

When the war ended, conditions changed yet again for women. As the soldiers returned, they were given back their old jobs. Some women left their positions voluntarily, but many weren't happy about being replaced. Four out of five women working in industry wanted to keep their jobs. A union delegate reported that in one shipyard,

98 percent of the women working there wanted to continue, or at least be able to use their skills.[46] The war industries paid good wages, thanks to the efforts of the unions. But after the war, the good wages and skilled industrial positions were basically closed to women.

Those who fought back by joining picket lines received little or no public sympathy. During the war, women had been recruited for nontraditional jobs and were cited for their contributions. In peacetime, a pervasive resentment surfaced, aimed at women who fought to keep their jobs. Even newspaper and magazine writers pressured women toward domestic lives. But gains had been made during the war. Some of the regulations that had restricted married women from entering the workforce were lifted. Eleven states and several unions sanctioned equal pay for equal work.[47] And women still continued to work; there were 16.5 million women working outside the home in 1950.[48]

During the postwar years, America's economy boomed. America's involvement in the Korean War in 1950 increased military production, and military spending peaked during the first half of the decade. The government was pouring money into public schools, housing, and interstate highways. By 1960, a third of the nation's population would live in the suburbs. As these suburbs expanded, the housing industry prospered. Roads had to be built and cars became necessities. This resulted in more jobs, and unemployment hovered at about 5 percent or lower. The prosperity encouraged single-income families, earlier marriages, and an increase in the birthrate.[49]

Challenging the Way Things Were

The postwar era was a time when women were encouraged to stay home and raise families. Suburban developments cropped up, and backyard barbeques became part of the weekend lifestyle. Day fashions became casual and comfortable.

Designer Claire McCardell provided American women with well-made, smart-looking casual American separates and was considered such an innovator that she appeared on the cover of *Time* magazine in 1955. McCardell emphasized comfort and classic lines, and her 1942 popover dress is a good example of her style. The popover was an inexpensive, attractive, denim wraparound dress that women could move in easily while they worked in their homes. McCardell also designed shorts, pants, short play dresses and skirts, and other sportswear, and constructed them so that women could swing a tennis racket or a golf club, ride a bike, or take a swim, and not feel constricted. She used good fabrics that held up.

Despite the general impression that this period was a domestic, quiet time for women, it really wasn't. There were women who were challenging unfair and long-established ways in many areas—from civil rights to employment practices and creative opportunities.

Rosa Parks, a quiet, respected, black community leader in Montgomery, Alabama, refused to give up her seat to a white person and move to the back of the bus in December 1955. Parks was arrested, which led to a mass boycott of the city's transit system by African-American residents. Parks's action on that day united African Americans to resist unfair racial practices. A year later, racial segregation of the public transportation system was ruled unconstitutional by the Supreme Court.

Women were beginning to actively protest discriminatory social conditions—in marches, demonstrations, and sit-ins. By the 1960s, women were also becoming involved in protests against war and nuclear weapons. In 1961, 50,000 women lobbied government officials during a one-day "strike," on the same day that airborne fallout from a Russian nuclear test started drifting across the country. In addition to the internal turmoil over issues of racial equality and civil rights, Americans also faced the possibility of a nuclear war. The threat was triggered by the "U-2 incident" when an American spy plane was cap-

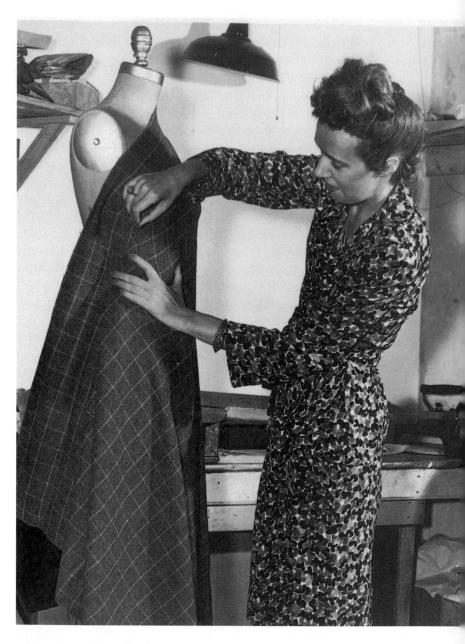

Designer Claire McCardell shaping fabric on a dress form

tured by the Soviet Union.[50] Some antiwar protests were led by a group of housewives who created a movement called the Women's Strike for Peace.

Around the same time, the baby boomers born in the postwar years came of age as college students. This group, more conscious of the world through the newly available medium of television, began questioning long-established values. Young women were also demonstrating for peace and racial equality. It wasn't practical to picket or march in stockings and heels, and fashions became less formal. Jeans, increasingly popular since the 1950s, became a youth symbol. They were comfortable and easy to move in and wear, and so were short skirts. As young people now made up a larger part of the population, fashions became more youth oriented. Mini dresses skimmed the body and were worn with low-heeled shoes. This non-constricting fashion allowed greater freedom and spontaneity.[51]

Fashion editor Diana Vreeland promoted these youthful styles. Vreeland was a fashion genius and an unusual woman. She came from a wealthy family and was imperious, witty, and smart. A top-notch fashion reporter and trendsetter during a twenty-four year stint as *Harper's Bazaar* editor, Vreeland then moved to *Vogue*, where she served as editor-in-chief from 1963 to 1971. "Mrs. Vreeland made *Vogue* the hottest magazine of its time," says Richard Martin, curator at the Costume Institute at the Metropolitan Museum of Art. "It evolved under her leadership and she made it into an exotic visual pleasure. She was the first managing editor to feature the human body. When she came on board, the fashion magazines were into a particular view of society and Mrs. Vreeland opened that up. The magazine became like a *National Geographic* and traveled around the world. She was one of the first to use black and Jewish models because she felt beauty was eclectic. It wasn't just traditional rarified beauty; there was a whole range of beauty."

Many designers are indebted to Vreeland; she used her power to promote them, gave them sound business advice, and connected them with people who could help them. Vreeland left *Vogue* while in her sixties, and from then until her death in 1989 she revolutionized the way a museum in the modern period could represent costume by creating dramatic and important fashion exhibitions at New York's Metropolitan Museum Art.

The last decades of the twentieth century have been a period of self-expression and personal freedom, in which women began wearing basically whatever they wanted and tossing what they didn't want—from girdles and, sometimes, bras to gloves, hats, and handkerchiefs.[52] A long flowing skirt with durable boots might be the look one day; bell-bottom pants with comfortable sandals might be an outfit the next.

The demonstrations that women organized and participated in during the 1960s and 1970s, including the massive 1968 march protesting the war in Vietnam, empowered women to seek a better world for themselves. On August 26, 1970, the fiftieth anniversary of the Nineteenth Amendment granting women the right to vote, women of all ages across the nation demonstrated in marches, teach-ins, and picket lines. This event was called the Strike for Equality, a demand for economic and social independence.[53] Like the working women of World War II, many of the participants wore pants and pant suits, feminine versions of men's attire, which became a form of women's take-charge expression in the 1970s.[54] Seventy-one pieces of legislation were passed during that decade, many in response to the Strike for Equality or to other issues to which women had committed themselves, to improve their lives.[55]

Part Two

Women Now

Fashion As an Industry

Pattern entrepreneur Nell Demorest, mill worker Harriet Robinson, garment worker Clara Lemlich, designer Liz Hawes, and all the other women who have worked in fashion laid the foundation for what the industry is today. It is now big business. According to 1995 statistics from the Department of Commerce, in that year Americans spent $116.4 billion on women's and children's clothing and accessories, more than a 50 percent jump from 1980.[1] The fashion industry is big in terms of jobs, too. In every state, more than one in eight people work in factories that produce textiles or garments for women, children, and men.[2] The major fashion centers are Los Angeles, Miami, Dallas, Chicago, Boston, Philadelphia, and New York City, which is the oldest and largest. In New York City alone, fashion is a $22 billion business that provides 180,000 jobs.[3]

What has been responsible for the fashion industry's growth? One reason is that fashion is now more accessible. In 1989, more than $30 billion of catalog apparel was purchased by Americans.[4] In 1993, more than half of all Americans ordered clothing by phone or mail.[5] Today, we also shop by television and through computer services, such as Prodigy.[6] In recent years, for example, women who clicked on the television set to QVC, one of the home shopping networks, were able to purchase designer Diane Von Furstenberg's Silk Assets and Casual Chic collections. Von Furstenberg, whose body-hugging wrap dresses were a sensation in department stores in the 1970s, adopted new marketing techniques in the 1990s to keep up with the times.[7]

Fashion has also became more newsworthy. In New York City during Fashion Week, a semi-annual event, designers unveil their spring and fall clothing collections for buyers. In the past, the shows were held in the designers' individual cramped showrooms. Beginning in 1993, many moved their runway shows to Bryant Park, a midtown location behind the New York Public Library. Fashion Week had always been exciting, but when many designer shows were held in the Bryant Park tents, it became a major event. About a thousand people, including buyers, celebrities, and VIPs flocked to first-day shows. The *New York Daily News* and the *New York Times*, *New Yorker* magazine, television's *Entertainment Tonight*, and other popular observers of the fashion scene all reported on the event called "7th on Sixth," derived from the Seventh Avenue addresses of many fashion businesses and the Sixth Avenue Bryant Park location.[8]

Who Works in the Fashion Industry?

When we look at a fashionable garment, what we see is the finished product. But before a garment is displayed in a department store, in a catalog, on QVC, or on a model in a runway show, it's already been in the making for at least one to two years. Along the way, many people contribute to its creation, each performing a specific job. Here are some of the basic steps.

A garment begins with fabric and that's what the tex-

Media photographers line the runway as Naomi Campbell and other models introduce a new collection at New York's Fashion Week.

tile industry supplies. Fibers of different kinds—cotton, wool, linen, synthetics, or others—are spun into yarns. These yarns are woven or knitted into fabric, and the fabric is finished with color, a pattern, or other features. Some manufacturers perform one process, such as spinning fibers into yarn; others perform all three and produce a finished fabric. There are about 2,500 textile plants in the country, employing more than 600,000 people. While the leading states in textile production still include New York, New Jersey, and Pennsylvania, production has shifted from the Northeast to the South. Their customers include clothing manufacturers, specific retail stores, privately owned shops, and designers who place orders. The design, styling, and sales staff for many of these mills are located in New York City.[9] For example, Milliken, a major fabric mill, has offices in New York and plants in Spartanburg, South Carolina.

Styling the Fabric

Let's look at a fabric stylist who works for a textile company. She has been researching the latest fabric trends. She chooses a variety of colors, including a vibrant gold as one of her samples for this season. Gold hasn't been a hot color for several years and perhaps it's a good time to introduce it again. The stylist has based her decisions on careful study; she reviewed the best- and worst-sellers of the previous season. She has also looked at the color projections made by the Color Association of the United States, a forecast service that providers subscribers with color predictions for two years into the future. The stylist has also had informal discussions with manufacturers, observed what is still lingering on their clothing racks and what's flying out of department stores, and paid attention to her gut feelings.[10] She has also selected the type of fabric, which can be soft and flowing like silk or rayon, or stiffer like denim or corduroy. She has made presentations and reports for her company, and management has approved her colors and fabric types.

Once the colors and fabric choices are firmly set, fabric designers step in. They think about what in-house or contracted machinery can be used to produce the proper weight and thickness for the material. If they have a beautiful print in mind, they must figure out whether the design will be too difficult to cut and sew because of the problem of matching up the print on the separate fabric pieces.[11]

After the fabric designer has settled on the plans, sample bolts of different fabric are produced for approval. When a sample is approved, a line (the season's collection of fabrics) is put together. Presentations, usually made by a mill's sales and merchandising staff, are given to the company's main clients, who get a first viewing of the fabrics about six months in advance of a season. The clients, including those who represent designer labels, are shown small fabric samples so they can see and touch the material, along with other sales aids. The presentation takes place at the client's showrooms or at the mill's. After the main clients are shown the new fabric lines, presentations are made to other customers, such as smaller apparel manufacturers.[12] Orders are placed for fabric for sample garments that will make up the season's collection.

Behind the scenes, there are other employees unknown to most people outside the business. A textile technologist tests the durability and colorfastness of a tough fabric that is being considered for outerwear. The material has stood up in countless washings, and the technologist makes an analysis of the findings and writes up a detailed report with recommendations. A fabric librarian updates her files, adding the latest seasonal presentations. In the afternoon, she plans to view another fabric line; the line's swatches might be a good resource for the library's collection.[13]

Once the fabric is in the hands of a designer, a garment begins to take shape. Still, there are well over a dozen major steps to go before a finished product is placed on a rack.[14]

Sketching a Collection

Most designers work for manufacturers of mass-produced clothing, and their challenge is to make good-looking garments that are affordable. Each designer usually has an assistant or a group of design-room helpers and one or two sample makers.[15] Designers generally create forty to seventy-five sketches for an upcoming season. These sketches, rough drafts in the beginning, eventually evolve into a series of well-defined drawings, a collection that has won the approval of the manufacturer.

A designer's job is probably the most admired and sought after in the fashion field, but it's not an easy one. Work days are usually long. Among other responsibilities, designers have to think about pricing, work closely with those sewing their creations, choose fabric and trim, and plan the work flow for their staff.[16] For a beginner to get a foot in the door is difficult, but there are ways. School internships provide some access. So may the ability to actually make a garment. Inma Medina, a Manhattan-based fashion designer in her early thirties, was a Fashion Institute of Technology intern for couture designer Carolina Herrera. Along with clerical duties, Medina also was given the chance to sew and drape. She feels her skill as a sewer helped her career. Medina gained a job with Herrera and later began her own couture business.[17]

After the designs are approved, a sample hand or expert seamstress makes up a garment. It is reviewed by a number of management people to determine how much it will cost, who can produce it, and what kind of profits it might make, along with other considerations.[18] If the garment receives approval, it's given a style number and is moved on to the next phase.

Designer Sarah Phillips (right) and a pattern maker watch as a sample hand puts the finishing touches on a new design.

Pattern makers

A pattern maker cuts master patterns out of hard paper for each piece of the garment, that is; sleeves, collar, skirt, and the rest. These patterns are then laid out on fabric, the fabric pieces are cut out and sewn together, and a garment is made.[19] It may need revisions, which will affect how much the total production will cost. When everyone agrees on what the garment should look like, another sample is made, usually by sample makers or duplicate hands. These samples—one-of-a-kind finished garments—are then put on display in the company showroom.[20]

Many small apparel companies use these display samples to show a season's new line. They invite buyers or people in the industry to their showroom for a preview. Larger, well-known companies and more prominent designers usually host a fashion show.

Lights, Cameras, Models

A fashion show—a glamorous display of the samples as worn by fashion models—requires planning, coordination, and timing. Usually a public relations person handles many of the details, and she can be an in-house employee or an employee of a public relations agency. She contacts a booker (a person who "books" or handles models' assignments) at a modeling agency well ahead of time—at least two months before the show, and much more if the desired model has celebrity status. She may, for some shows, arrange for live music; one of designer Donna Karan's shows included the New York City Church of Christ gospel choir.[21] She may also hire a director and a music coordinator; a fashion show has a certain flow that may require choreography as the models walk to the musical beat. Press releases are developed and invitations are sent to fashion editors and reporters; exposure in a major newspaper or magazine is good promotion. Every detail of the show must be fine-tuned, including the plan for guest seating.

But the buyers and merchandisers are the people designers most want to see. These potential clients, who purchase fashions for department stores, small shops, or catalogs, might place large orders.[22]

Producing Fashion

Once a buyer places an order, say an order of 100 to 500 pieces, the garment goes into production. A pattern grader (or the pattern maker) adapts the master pattern to cre-

Lighting, music, choreography, and models—in
addition to the designer's collection—are some of the
elements of a successful fashion show.

ate patterns for every size in the company's line. This task
requires precision because a quarter-inch mistake can
ruin the whole size.[23] Markers then make the pattern outlines for each size on a long paper guide, arranging the
outlines so that a minimum of fabric is wasted. Spreaders
carefully lay out long bolts of the fabric, constantly
smoothing the material as it is unfolded. Using electric
cutting machines, knives, or shears, cutters follow the pattern outline as a guide to cut through the thick piles of

material. These cut fabric pieces are now bundled and taken to sewing operators.

Some operators may work on sleeves only; others may work on just buttonholes. The work involves dexterity, concentration, and stamina. A good operator checks to make sure that important details are produced correctly; for example, seams should be straight, darts should be flat and even. Once a full garment is produced, a finisher checks for loose threads or lint.[24]

Production managers are responsible for getting the shipment finished on schedule. The manager hires the workers and plans schedules, and also oversees machinery maintainance, the performance of quality checks, and the cost-efficiency of production methods.[25]

The finished garments are then inspected, pressed, and packaged for delivery.[26] More than 22,000 companies make clothing nationwide. Some of these companies do everything themselves—from designing the garment through to producing a finished product. In other companies, some functions are managed inside the company while other funtions are contracted out.[27]

Promoting the Look

You may have seen a newspaper photograph of one of the dresses a designer has introduced. A well-written article by the fashion editor of your favorite magazine states that you can wear the dress for a business meeting, as well as for a dinner date. It's fitted but not confining, fully lined, and affordable. It seems perfect. Before choosing to show and describe that dress, the editor scheduled an appointment with the designer. The editor probably met with other designers to look at their lines, too. Deciding that this dress looked like one her readers would like, she scheduled a fashion shoot.

A fashion photographer who took the picture at the shoot captured the vivid color and style of the dress. The process took eight hours or more, including setting up lighting equipment, pauses to touch up the model's make-up, and to direct her so that the dress and its accessories were in clear view. Hundreds of shots were taken before one was chosen.

The model wearing the dress looks spirited, classy, and fresh, even though she posed for hours in a drafty location. She had posed for another shoot the day before in a different locale, and that was pretty tiring. But the model is a professional and has managed to convey a look you like. So you head for the dress in your favorite local department store, part of a well-known chain.

In the Store

When you enter the store, before you get to the dress department, here's what you see. There's a sparkling glass cosmetics counter up front. Cosmetics are usually a store's most profitable department, so they are almost always placed near a front door entrance. So are jewelry, scarves, and handbags. Beautiful silk scarves and leather bags carefully arranged in a glass display case signal luxury. That means they're expensive. Still, an attractively displayed bag and scarf might strike you as the perfect accessories for that dress you want, and you might ask to look at them. These are known as impulse items because they are aimed at catching your attention to entice you into buying them—while you're on your way to another purchase.[28]

You might pass "dump bins," tables that display small items such as gloves and leather goods. The dump bins are another sales aid designed to stop you. Many times, sale goods and bargains are piled on tables or in bins, so you think that there might be a bargain here. Sometimes there is, but not today.[29]

Next, you enter the dress department. It's close to the front of the store, and the designer dress you're searching for is on the very first rack. The display looks brand new because it is; the shipment was put out early this morning. Just a few days ago, on your last visit, these racks showed a different outfit. One reason the new dress is prominently displayed is that stores profit the most on sales of new merchandise.[30]

Retailing

A buyer from the department store decided to order that dress you like. Someone else tagged it and put it on the rack. Another staff person decided to rearrange the designer dress department so that it looked more glamorous. And yet another searched for the right handbag and scarf to coordinate with that dress. Who are the retail people responsible for all this?

The buyer or department head of designer wear, working from the chain's headquarters, selected the dress you want to buy. She was given a budget to spend for this season, and this was one of the lines she ordered. She has already met with the store's sales staff to point out the specific features and details that may clinch a sale. As a matter of fact, she may have spoken to you when you were looking at the dress. Buyers know it's important to find out what customers want and to see what they buy, and so they visit various local stores in the chain to do this.[31]

It's also important for buyers to see what's on the market. Buyers travel to the other fashion centers in several major cities and sometimes overseas. They look at the merchandise other stores are selling and read scores of fashion forecasts and trend reports.

One of the industry's forecast aids is the *Tobé Report*. Tobé Coller Davis was the first fashion coordinator in the 1920s for Franklin Simon, once a major department store.[32] She started the *Tobé Report*, a merchandising trend service that provides a clear, extensive update on trends

Attractive displays of well-chosen and accessorized
styles are important in retailing fashion.

and fads. The attractively produced report, which con-
tains no advertising, is packed with 80 to 100 pages of
editorial material, illustrations, and photos, as well as
accompanying style numbers, wholesale prices, and the
names of the manufacturers. Your store has subscribed to
this service, one of several forecast services available.[33]

The buyer also pours over *Women's Wear Daily*, another long-time, well-known industry aid. *Women's Wear
Daily*, with its subheading *The Retailer's Daily Newspaper*,
is a fashion newspaper in tabloid form. It has the latest

hard news and features about fashions, the department stores, designers, trends, markets, and the major fashion centers, as well as a classified section for jobs.

Buyers also review the store's inventories on a daily basis—to see what is selling, and what isn't. It's a big responsibility. The buyer's purchasing decisions can determine the success of a department. If a department produces profits, the store thrives.[34]

The buyer reports to the merchandise manager. A merchandise manager usually has several buyers reporting to her; for example, buyers for designer, dressy, and better dresses may staff her department. Years of contacts with manufacturers and suppliers help the manager guide her buyers in these markets. She must be aware of new sources and that involves travel to seek them out. It means looking over a manufacturer's dresses for quality, asking questions about the kinds of materials used, how much the dresses will cost to produce, and how quickly they can be delivered. If you noticed that the store's designer dress department was set up differently from other departments, more like a boutique, the merchandise manager was most likely responsible for that. She also usually oversees training for the buyers and their assistants, for salespeople and for merchandise clerks. It's a job with many responsibilities.[35]

Remember the scarf and bag that coordinated with your dress? The store is also showing a pair of shoes to complement the look, as well as hose, jewelry, gloves, and a hat. Someone planned ahead so that these accessories were coordinated and available, not only for your new dress, but for every outfit in the store. That person is the fashion coordinator. While a buyer is involved with a specific line of apparel, such as designer dresses, the fashion coordinator reviews trends and makes sure that the whole store reflects a common theme. Her job involves doing projections of color, trends, and fabrics several months ahead of a season and making presentations that include illustrations and other visuals of the merchandise that she feels should be in stock. She works with the store's merchandising managers and buyers.[36] She has a voice in the store's advertising plans, and if the store hosts a fashion show, she makes all the arrangements—from the clothing and accessories to models and publicity.[37]

Your new dress was shipped to your local store from the chain's central warehouse. Before it was placed on the rack, someone had already recorded such things as the size, style number, color, and department. That person attached a price tag to it, and carefully hung it on the rack according to size. That person was the merchandise clerk. The buyer relies on inventory numbers to assess how a line is selling, so accurate record keeping is an important part of the merchandise clerk's job.[38]

The saleswoman who helped you find the right size rings up your purchase at the register. She takes the ticket and scans it into the register's computer system. That ticket, which includes the manufacturer, style number, department, size, and price has valuable information. For example, if the designer dress you just purchased is a sell-out in all sizes, cumulatively, those tickets prove that the color, style, size, and—ultimately—the manufacturer are a hit.

But it may be a hit only in your part of the country. In another area, this dress doesn't do as well. Or in another, larger sizes sell and the smaller ones don't.[39] All this information is studied. It helps retail people decide what market, or group of people, will buy a style or color, and how they can stock their stores more efficiently. It helps them determine what to push for future seasons. This feedback is also used by the textile companies and clothing manufacturers, as well as the designer of your new dress.

The positions and activities we've mentioned here are only a selection of the many, many different fashion jobs that women fill. They work in a wide range of other areas:

producing copy for catalog companies; advising and selecting clothing for busy women as personal shoppers; creating advertising campaigns; working in the leather, fur, and millinery industries. In the following pages, a number of successful fashion women give us a glimpse of what their fashion careers are like. They describe their journeys, with setbacks and challenges. And they talk about what events and decisions helped them become leaders in their fields.

Women Working in the Fashion Industry

CAROLINA HERRERA, COUTURE FASHION DESIGNER

The sun streams through the windows of Carolina Herrera's rooftop office, a harmoniously decorated light-filled place. Cream-colored walls, carpet, and drapes edged in brown, striking cocoa-accented pillows and throws, tiered plants in clay pots, and tables with stacks of books make up the polished decor. Herrera is beautiful, gracious, vibrant, as she talks about her past and present. From time to time, she picks up one of many silver-framed photos and points out family members. "I grew up with all very elegant women, all very well dressed women. That helps the eye, no?" Carolina Herrera asks that question with a smile, crediting her heritage for her design success.

The elegant women she refers to, her mother, grandmother, and mother-in-law, were all wealthy members of Caracas, Venezuela, society and clients of great couturiers such as Cristobel Balenciaga, Christian Dior, and Elsa Schiaparelli. Herrera has gone further, becoming a creator of fashion. Her company's sales volume for 1994 was

Fashion designer, Carolina Herrera

$8 million in retail, $15 million through licensed products.[1]

Herrera's childhood revolved around horses, dogs, and tennis. "I didn't have my own way of dressing," she recalls of her strict upbringing. "I was *ordered* to dress a certain way. We all wore little white dresses and proper shoes," she explains, the "we" a reference to her three sisters. Style, taste, and elegant details were introduced early. At thirteen, her grandmother took Herrera in hand to view the designs of the great Balenciaga in Paris. It was her first fashion show. "Even if I wasn't thinking 'fashion,' it still surrounded me."

Fashion shows then, in the 1950s, were very different from those of today, she explains. "The shows were very quiet. There was no music, it was all very small, and took place in ateliers. There was no runway and people sat along the side in chairs to watch the models as they came out. Then, the models were anonymous. Now, if there is no 'face,' people don't want to come; sometimes the dresses don't count. In those days, that wasn't the case." She pauses and looks over for emphasis, her posture erect. "The model was at eye level. You were looking at the workmanship and beauty and simplicity of the clothes. That was impressive."

Attention to detail is a valuable, necessary trait for a designer or for anyone who wants to succeed in life, and Herrera learned this early on. "My mother was very artistic," says Herrera. "She had all her values in place. She was very straight and we were close. She always said that both women and men should be cultivated. Poetry was read aloud. We had to read and she took us to museums. We couldn't just glance at a picture, we had to really look at it and remember what made it so special. She always said that the details in life were important."

As a young woman, Herrera brought her first designs—little sketches and suggestions—to her local dressmaker. "I had a very good seamstress," she remembers. "I would buy material and go to her and say, 'could we mix these two fabrics,' or if the skirts were very long, I wanted them very short." When she started expressing her fashion sense, Herrera was a busy mother of four daughters—two from an early marriage and two from a longtime union with Reinaldo Herrera. She was an internationally known beauty who was frequently featured in the style pages wearing designer clothes. But friends began talking about her own styles as well. "I wore one dress, the top was black velvet," she recalled. "It had a full brown taffeta skirt with a big black velvet bow in the back and I wore it to a Diana Vreeland exhibit at the Metropolitan Museum of Art. A friend said, 'What a beautiful dress.'" The friend was French designer Yves Saint Laurent. "That gave me an idea that maybe I should go into business for myself."

Herrera designed twenty dresses and had them made in Venezuela. Then she brought them here. One of the first people to see the collection was *Vogue* fashion editor Diana Vreeland, a supporter who had long admired Herrera's fashion sense and encouraged her to create her own designs. Herrera contacted buyers from prominent stores including Saks, Martha's, Bergdorf Goodman, and found they wanted to buy her clothing. Herrera found a backer, Armondo de Armas, head of a South American publishing company, and set up Carolina Herrera, Ltd. Friends such as well-established designers Bill Blass and Emanuel Ungaro gave Herrera tips, and she launched her first show at the Metropolitan Club, a private club in New York City, in 1981.

The show was a glamorous affair with live music and Cole Porter songs. Herrera's designs—fitted, sculpted, feminine fashions—were a contrast to the layers of sweaters and droopy skirts that were the trend at the time.

Was she nervous? "I was hysterical," she answers immediately. "I had butterflies choking me inside," she puts her hands to her throat. "But I didn't show it on the outside, I never do. If I did, then everyone would be the same way." About 500 people turned out for the event, but the reviews were "quite bad" as she puts it. "I had to prove myself," she says candidly. "Some of the newspaper writers predicted, 'she's going to do it for only one or two seasons,' or said 'you don't need to work.' Why do you need to do work? Why can't you do it because you want to?"

But her clothes were a hit where they counted, with the women who bought them. Herrera's debut collection became one of Saks Fifth Avenue's best-sellers, with staying power right through the end of the season without price markdowns—an amazing feat as her luncheon suits averaged $3,000.[2, 3]

Jackie Onassis and Nancy Reagan became fans of Herrera's fashions; thick file binders with their names and those of other private clients stand on shelves in a pantry-like closet within the main design room. She added a more affordable line in 1986, CH by Carolina Herrera. A bridal collection was launched in 1987, after Caroline Kennedy chose her to design a wedding gown.

"In the beginning, I didn't know where the business would go. I didn't think there would be so much work. You have to like it very much because it's a very tough job," Herrera admits. While she knew about taste, design, and appeal, the nuts and bolts of a business—organizing production and being on time with deliveries—had to be nailed down. In the past, Herrera has denied any credit for business acumen, but she had enough vision to hire talented, creative people such as business manager Michael Pellegrino, her chief executive officer and managing director, who guided the company's growth and, along with Herrera, helped develop a close-knit organization.[4]

Herrera likes being surrounded by young people and the atmosphere is calm, relaxed, and productive. There's a reciprocal affection from the staffers she warmly greets and introduces in the design and sample rooms and administrative offices; many of them have been with Herrera about ten years.[5]

In one of her showrooms, she pulls out a dramatic purple suit priced just under $200 from her Studio collection. "These are 'bridge,'" she says. Bridge clothing is high priced, but lower than designer fashions, and is designed to appeal to a wider market.

Her stamp, Herrera says, is on everything, including her licensed products: knitwear collections, coats, eyewear,

Two elegant designs from a recent Herrera collection

costume jewelry, handbags, and accessories. (Licensing is a legal arrangement. A specific manufacturer has the right to use a designer's name for a certain amount of time on certain designated goods it makes.) "When the fragrance company approached me about licensing a personal line, they asked me, 'what do you want?'" Herrera explained about the development of the fragrance line that bears her name. She chose jasmine and tuberose, a signature fragrance she'd been mixing together herself for years. "It took two years to develop the right combination," she says. "Sometimes I would wear a sample and people would ask me if I was wearing a different fragrance, so I would have them mix it again."

She keeps track of everything through organization. Working with the best materials, aiming for allure, pure lines, and simplicity are her aspirations. "Excess for me is the worst," she says emphatically.

Herrera's office opens for business promptly at 9:00 A.M. "Sometimes I come in early, sometimes I come to work later," she says. "But I never work past five." Herrera means it; she has often commented, "If you can't get it done by five, you're not doing it right." That applies to all sixty employees; from the people who work at her headquarters as well as the crew sewing the fashions in the factory a block away.

CLAIRE ORTIZ, RETAILER

Claire Ortiz takes no breathers between challenges. This former design director for Esprit clothing for young juniors led the creation of a 300-piece clothing line from design to finished product while juggling a daunting travel schedule. She left the well-known San Francisco–based junior sportswear company in June 1995. With her next step in mind, Ortiz aimed for her own retail store and clothing line with partner Joanne Dolan. The store, named

"415" for San Francisco's area code, opened for business in October the same year.

"The week after I left Esprit, I began scouting out a place and put together a plan of what I needed financially to run the business the first year. I can't do anything *but* work," says Ortiz in her second floor office on Filbert Street in San Francisco's Pacific Heights area[6]. Her headquarters, a 1895 carriage house painted turquoise, stands out on a street of white residential and commercial structures.

Ortiz and Dolan invested equal funds rather than rely on a backer. "The whole reason to start this business was to be free of anyone else," explains Ortiz candidly. "The most important thing for us was that we were free to run the business as we saw fit. It defeated that purpose if we were to bring in a financial person or sign for a bank loan."

It took two weeks to find the building, a former bed and breakfast inn. "It was literally a dungeon," says Ortiz. "The upstairs was painted all in brown. Just imagine, brown ceilings," she adds wryly. With the current cheerful interior—1,000 square feet of bright yellow walls and vibrant blue stairs with stenciled gold stars—it's hard to visualize the drab mess that Ortiz and Dolan tackled. Ortiz describes her efforts: "Every day I left the house dressed in overalls and steel-toed boots, with all of my tools. We scraped the walls and the floors, painted, put in lighting fixtures, built the shelves and dressing rooms ourselves."

Ortiz's partner, Dolan, is a former mechandise planner for Esprit. Of their working styles Ortiz comments, "We're left brain, right brain—I'm creative, Joanne is numbers. She decides how many items we need to sell by the end of the month, how much merchandise we need to order, how much the store needs to make. We shop the market together and go to New York trade shows, boutique shows, shows in Los Angeles, and we put together a color scheme. We're changing every month, sometimes every six weeks. I always want black and navy as basics, for spring we add pastels and brights." They generally carry 2,000 items, including a full line of accessories.

Their aim is to offer affordable clothing, and they show designers such as Betsey Johnson and Joan Stewart, as well as their own line, "415." A quarter of the merchandise is trendy; the rest, Ortiz says, can be worn by anyone. "It's geared for the active, professional woman. We get a lot of ad executives, legal people, artists. They tell us, 'I don't want a suit that's constricting. I want comfort.' So we try to put color, fun, and life in the pieces. For spring we have knits, striped jerseys, silks, and linen. Our fall line will carry nylon, polyester blends, pearlized fabrics, and things with texture." Ortiz expected the store's "415" clothing line, sold exclusively in-house at first, to be carried in other retail stores by the fall of 1996.

What does Ortiz do in the store besides planning what merchandise to carry, the color schemes, and styles? "It's a lot of phone work," Ortiz admits. "I'm often on the phone with vendors ordering piece goods and inventory. Then, I constantly review orders coming in. If they're late, I'll call to find out when I'll get it, and if I'll get a discount. I also help customers, put people into dressing rooms, run up sales."

Being your own boss doesn't mean the days are shorter. Ortiz gets in at 10:00 A.M. and leaves the store at 8:00 P.M. "At Esprit, it was more like 8 to 8. If anything though, I'm even more excited about what I do. I love this business. I always wanted my own store and my own line," she says. Ortiz, who admits to being a perfectionist, had Esprit's upcoming fall and winter line ready to go when she left the company. "I left on good terms. Working for Esprit was a steppingstone. It was also an incredible experience," says Ortiz.

That it was. For twenty weeks a year, Ortiz traveled all over the world visiting cotton mills and denim and trim factories. "Sometimes I felt like a photojournalist," she says. "I went everywhere, including a lot of Third World countries. I drove over rough, primitive roads through jungles to look at a sewing factory in Peru guarded by fourteen-year-old boys with machine guns." Ortiz's travel also enabled her to forecast fashion in the States, and her tool was a handheld video camera. By filming teenagers at restaurants and clubs in Los Angeles, New York, San Francisco, Dallas, and Chicago, Ortiz chronicled the shifting youthful trends. These videos and the dance club flyers she collected were edited into a fifteen-minute, low-budget film. Ortiz's street observations influenced her designs and served as a pitch to her sales team four times a year. "My approach was a little unconventional," she admits. "But I tried to pinpoint where the trends were coming from. When I showed an entire group of satin skirts and the sales team moaned and said, 'Oh my God,' I ran film clips of kids buying vintage satin in secondhand stores. The average fourteen-year-old isn't into the Paris collection. They think about what their hair looks like and which concert tickets to buy. And if there's a rap group with a gold record, that group is going to be influential. You had to get out there and pay attention to what 20 million kids were doing."

Ortiz's fashion path has been unconventional. Her father is a Cherokee, her mother is African American, and the family was dirt-poor, moving from Texas, to Oklahoma, and Kansas, during her high school years. A political science major at Georgetown University, Ortiz dropped out in her junior year to pursue design. "I had no idea what a design school was," says Ortiz. "My mother freaked out when I left Georgetown and told me 'you can't make money in clothing.'" Ortiz basically learned her work from the bottom up. She found her first design job by answering an ad for a designer's assistant in *California Apparel News*. "I got the job. It was for a small cruisewear company, and they moved me to New York from Los Angeles," she recalls chuckling, "but what I basically did was count and ship clothing." After three months, Ortiz returned to Los Angeles and took another designer's assistant job. The second position was more promising and more hands-on. Ortiz was involved with aspects such as sketching. She also calculated details that included how much fabric it took to make a garment, how many buttons were needed, and planned the schedule in the sewing room.

It's been an interesting journey for Ortiz, who recalls the teen years with her family as a welfare recipient. "I don't buy into 'I'm poor and I am what I am,'" she says frankly. "Now I'm pretty glad I had my upbringing. Because I don't take anything for granted."

EVE FEUER, FASHION DIRECTOR

Studio 536 sits between Tenth and Eleventh Avenues on West Twenty-ninth Street in New York City. Surrounded by warehouses, the exterior fits into the stark New York area. But inside, the industrial atmosphere fades away as a crew prepares a fantasy, using lights, cameras, makeup, clothing, and a beautiful model. There's even a little intrigue. Seven hundred thousand dollars worth of diamond and gold jewelry is being protected by a security guard. Eve Feuer, fashion director at *New Woman* magazine is in charge of the activity. Her assignment: create a retro theme, reminiscent of the 1940s, with spring suits for the magazine's April issue.

Feuer's been there since 9:00 A.M. "There's a lot of waiting," Feuer says resolutely, heading upstairs toward the tiny fitting room. Manicure, makeup, hair styling were all begun before the fittings started at 11:15 A.M. Now, the slender, energetic Feuer inspects sleeve and skirt length, fit, and overall impact as the model steps in and out of glamorous suits by DKNY, Norma Kamali, Zelda,

Eve Feuer, fashion director

Giuseppe, and CK Calvin Klein that teeter around the
$800 range. "Are you cold?" jokes the photographer
Christopher Micaud as the model shivers a little in her
clothing. "You're lucky," comments Feuer wryly, as the
January temperature holds at thirty-five degrees outside.
"Chris wanted to shoot at an airport hangar."

After lunch, a comb-out, and makeup touch-up, the
model is ready. The backdrop is a white concrete construction called a cyclorama—basically a wide, deep floor
that gently curves up to a wall on one side. Tungsten lights
flood the scene, creating a soft, 1940s movie glow. The

photographer's Pentax 67 camera rests on a tripod ready to go, but he takes some Polaroid shots first. It's a warm-up for the model, who sits on a curved sofa, and a test run for shadows and best angles, as well as a check to ensure that accessories show up. The makeup person zooms in between takes, powdering the model's hands to eliminate any redness. Sometimes Feuer stands in back of Chris, watching. Sometimes she confers with her staff or the magazine's creative director, Ann Kwong. "We need to do something with her hair," she comments. Or she'll go over to the model to adjust the pants and jacket, or a button, as the photographer changes film. Booker T and the MGs play softly in the background and the atmosphere is relaxed. It takes an hour to photograph the first suit.[7]

"We were there until nine o'clock that night," says Feuer in her office a week later. "It doesn't usually take that long but we started with a manicure, and the hair and makeup went a little slow so it blew the whole morning." Otherwise, no glitches, which doesn't happen all the time. Sometimes the clothing doesn't fit the model and Feuer has to scramble for quick replacements from designers.[8]

For the end result, Feurer scrutinized roughly 200 shots for each of the suits featured. "There was a time crunch here, so Chris made up a contact sheet, instead of developing each print which he usually does. He marks his choices, then I look them over, then Ann reviews them. We're all looking at different things, that's why it's a collaborative effort. When Chris edits, he's looking at things like expression and composition. I'm looking at whether or not the clothes look wrinkled, if the shoes show up. Ann looks at the overall picture. In this case, we liked the model's smiles more than Chris did because we need more approachable women."

Feuer directs two fashion shoots a month. She's responsible for the all-important magazine cover plus ten pages of fashion in each issue, except for March and

September, when her section expands a bit to twelve pages as a showcase for spring and fall fashions. "We're not a fashion magazine, so we have a small staff and we get to do everything. But that's good because I'm involved in every part of the shoot and it's fulfilling," Feuer says. That includes choosing studios, designers, casting, and hair and makeup people, as well as deciding on fashion story ideas. An associate pulls the accessories together and three assistants book hair, makeup, models, clothing, and appointments with designers. To get ready for a shoot, Feuer visits showrooms every day for a week at half-hour intervals, aiming her camera at the fashions she likes, sometimes seeing ten designers in one day. Then it's back in the office to write copy, or maybe review her associate's shoot.

This is a dream job for Feuer. But she didn't arrive at this point in her life easily. During her twelve-year career, she freelanced as a fashion stylist for MTV, Macy's Juniors, Lifetime Television, Coca-Cola, and Ellen Tracy, as well as well-known catalogs such as those from Bloomingdale's and Talbots. Feuer attended Boston College, where she signed up for pre-law courses. "I always liked fashion, but I was kind of a snob about it, thinking it wasn't serious enough as a career," she says. Feuer found out about summer retailing classes at the Fashion Institute of Technology and took them. After graduation, she worked in her family's leather business as a fashion coordinator.

Feuer's first editorial job was as market editor for a trade publication called *Sportswear International,* and she quickly became its fashion director, hiring stylists, photographers, and everyone else needed for a fashion shoot. "It came out eight times a year, but it had about a hundred pages of photography," she said. "We worked every night until 9:00 P.M. and on weekends, and after two years, I had enough." That's when Feurer began freelancing as a stylist. "It depends on the client," she says, explaining the responsibilities. "Maybe you pick up the shoes and the accessories and schedule the shoots for each day. Talbots would schedule the shoots. Bloomingdale's did all the casting. You have to know little tricks to make the clothing fit properly."

Along her fashion path was a two-year stint with *Harper's Bazaar* as a fashion editor, where she traveled extensively to Europe, Africa, St. Barts. "At *Bazaar*, I learned how a real fashion department is run," she says. "I worked with some great people and learned the art of diplomacy that you need at a shoot. There's always a give and take with photographers." Feuer says she keeps an inspiration file of black and white photos she likes and attends photography exhibits when she has the time.

TRACY REESE, FASHION DESIGNER

The members of the *Entertainment Tonight* camera crew drag their tripods and equipment into the Celeste Forum, a small, elegant room in the New York Public Library, a half hour before the fashion show, which is part of "7th on Sixth," begins. Gold-colored cane chairs labeled *Women's Wear Daily, Marie Claire, New York Times,* and *Vogue* flank both sides of the runway. The sound mixer punches the air as energetic music swirls out from gigantic speakers, staff members in red and black dart around making last-minute preparations, and uniformed security guards walk around with walkie-talkies. Colored lights transform the white wall in front of the runway into a palette of peach and lavender, spotlighting the designer's name in block letters: Tracy Reese for Magaschoni.[9]

It's New York Fashion Week and the New York Public Library is hosting the event within its beautiful, stately walls as well as in tents behind the building in adjoining Bryant Park. The event is a major one; the industry's top designers put on fifty-one shows between Sunday and

Friday, staged mostly for buyers and journalists, and about 2,500 are expected to turn out to see the new ready-to-wear trends.[10] Reese's show is standing-room-only; the 500 seats are all taken, and people lined up two and three deep crane from the back. The orchestrated half-hour display of fashions and fantasy is fun; the audience cheers and claps as a model with attitude in a movie-

Tracy Reese, fashion designer

star-like white pantsuit struts down the ramp with a trailing porter carrying her luggage. A piano version of "Sophisticated Lady" with a lush string background plays, as models stride out in knockout sleeveless, V-necked sheath dresses in dove gray and pink reminiscent of the 1950s. Marilyn Monroe sings "We're Having a Heat Wave," while a model in a tomato red body-hugging gown undulates, and Prince's cheeky "You Don't Have to Be Rich, to Be My Girl" accompanies a model in a white satin pantsuit with red-sequined lip prints on the jacket. The clothes—elegant, feminine and drop-dead gorgeous—weren't created without a lot of effort; a staffer mentions that seamstresses were working on the creations until 7:00 that morning.

"The schedule is murder just before a show," Reese admits afterwards.[11] "We were working until midnight every day, including weekends a month before. And everyone was involved, the whole staff and interns, because anything we want to develop quickly we have to do ourselves." Reese began designing the clothes in April, for the November 1 show, which required some long-distance juggling because the company's sample room, where the clothing is made, is in Hong Kong. "Anything I needed, I had to get out of Hong Kong at least a month before the show," she explains. And that was just the clothing. The show's theme, music, and choreography had to be developed, a two-month project.

Three weeks later, Reese still isn't enjoying a lull. She had been up the previous night sketching the next fall line. "We're so busy with the spring production, appointments with editors and buyers during the day," she says, referring to the steady stream outside. "And once I get into a groove, I can't stop."

There were ninety-two different outfits in her spring collection, in beautiful, fluid fabrics mostly from Italy and Paris; silk georgette and shantungs, as well as boucles, metallic knits, and crepes. That was just one line, and this was Reese's third Public Library show. Where do her ideas come from? "It's a lot of things," she says thoughtfully. "There are so many influences that come together. At the Premier Vision Fabric Fair in Paris, which takes place twice a year, I get an overall feel for fabric, clothing, and textures and put them together for the company. And spring always rings that bell for me. I was looking to make good, classic things new somehow and thought it was time to get back to real clothing. Finally, I got into the lightness, prettiness, and femininity of the season."

Reese has since left Magaschoni, an amicable agreement that Reese says was timely.[12] "I'd worked with them for five years, and had been seriously considering it," she says from her New York apartment. "What I wasn't comfortable with was the push to be bridge, those fashions that have to be broad-based in look and fit. I wanted to stay more specialized." Reese is in the midst of looking for a working partner, developing a business plan, and conducting market research for her new company, but she has a great head start. Her name under the Magaschoni label was carried by large, upscale department stores such as Bloomingdale's, Nieman Marcus, Saks, and Henri Bendel, as well as about a hundred specialty stores around the country. Reese and her clothing have even made film appearances; she was featured in a cameo role in *White Man's Burden*, a film released in December 1995 starring Harry Belafonte and John Travolta. Happily, Reese was typecast; she played a designer at a charity fashion show.

A gracious, articulate woman, Reese, who grew up in a family of five children, traces her fashion interest to her mother, grandmother, and her Detroit surroundings. "My mom was a big home sewer," she recalls with a smile, "and my grandmother is very fashionable. Whenever she sends a snapshot, she's well put together, right down to the gloves. Also in Detroit, it's still important to dress there. When people go to the theater, they dress up. When they go to a concert, they dress up. It's a whole different attitude to clothing. When I go home, people are wearing all sorts of color."

Reese didn't initially think of clothing design as a career. "I figured I'd take liberal arts, or architecture and interior design in college," she says. She credits her alma mater, Cass Tech High School, a public school in Detroit, for sparking her talent; it was there that she took her first fashion design courses. But it was a summer scholarship between junior and senior years at Parsons School of Design that clinched Reese's career path. "That's what made me excited," she says candidly. "When I realized I could be a businessperson and a designer, that made it much more challenging."

Her first job was assistant designer to Martine Sitbon, an avant-garde designer for Arlequin. She worked there for three years. "If there's one thing I remember about that first job, it was the speed at which we worked; we had to put a whole season together in a week," she says. "We had to leave the office to do sketches and would go to my boss's apartment and sketch for hours. We'd sit there and sketch all kinds of things." Reese laughs. "The joke was, if it wound up being ugly, we had to wear it for a year." Reese struck out on her own for a couple of years and was the sole employee of her own company. "My dad backed me. It was very difficult," she says, "but a lot of young designers were doing the same thing. I sold to Barneys, Bergdorf's, and other good stores, and then the market crashed." She spent a year designing for Perry Ellis before Magaschoni called.

Reese looks at old movies when she has the time, but even then it's in search of design ideas. And she's passionate about books, which she uses for inspiration and reference. "I buy tons and tons of books on flowers, interiors, and fabric. And I must have at least seven books on lingerie," she says. She's also an involved Parsons School of Design alumna. Marie Essex, chair of fashion design at Parsons School of Design, remembers Reese as a vibrant student who was a natural in her design illustration class. "She came in with fabulous skills. She knew how to paint, and color, and draw, and was very capable of projecting designs on paper with ease. I still have her croquis books (designer's idea books). And she was so prolific. Tracy could do terrific children's clothes as well as sophisticated clothes and that's important."[13]

As a senior, Reese's croquis books were critiqued by her teachers. Now she's critiquing students. "I like working with students," says Reese. "It's important that they become more familiar with the industry. Because it's not what they think."

HUNTER RENO, FASHION MODEL

A tall, striking young woman with tousled, short blonde hair, cornflower blue eyes, and a flawless complexion breezes into the coffee shop. There's a warm, direct greeting, a firm handshake, and a candid aside as she waits to order her café au lait. "I'm still trying to get the hang of this," says Hunter Reno, glancing down at her footwear. "Katherine Hepburn wears socks and sandals and she's my idol." She looks as if she's got it. Reno carries off her socks, sandals, jeans, black tee, and crisp white shirt with the athletic, confident style of the legendary star. Reno sits gracefully in a chair by a window, and her fresh look softens the dreary, November day outside. Reno, a top model with the Elite agency, had left the profession for two years, then returned at age twenty-six.[14]

"Becoming a model was not my initial idea," she says, cradling her coffee cup. Reno talks about growing up in southern Florida, scurrying up trees and sailing in her dad's small boat to the Bahamas. "We tested all the barriers in nature," she says smiling, recalling the good times with her brother. A photo of Reno's suntanned good looks

Fashion model, Hunter Reno

at thirteen caught the interest of her mother's friend, who suggested they send it to a modeling agency in New York. "The thing I remember most," she says of her career choice, "is thinking, 'if you don't do it now, it won't happen.'"

Reno and her mother flew to New York for a two-week stay, eventually approaching Eileen Ford, head of one of the best-known modeling agencies. "My mom went in and said to the receptionist, 'you've turned down the photo we've sent, but we were in the neighborhood,'" she remembers. Reno was enthusiastic and personable and came across well. The agency receptionist connected them with a booker. In a week and a half, Reno was hired for her first shoot; a before-and-after makeover for *Co-Ed* magazine.

Reno eventually signed with Elite, her current agency. She owns her own apartment now, but in the beginning she stayed in a two-room apartment crammed with bunk beds that housed eight models, a standard residence for novices. "Here I was without a sister suddenly living with girls who ranged in age from thirteen to twenty. It was pretty dynamic and I learned what competition was, which I was used to athletically, in a different setting." The young model paid $350 a week for the room, plus expenses.

The newcomer's first magazine cover was *Mademoiselle*. Reno was fifteen. They were heady times for Reno, who attended high school in Miami and flew up on weekends for big clients such as *Vogue, Mademoiselle,* and *Self.* Reno lived in New York during the summers, then for a whole year while she attended Professional Children's School, a school geared to students in show business and modeling. She worked with top-echelon photographers such as Richard Avedon and Bill King. "No one's ever duplicated what he had," she says admiringly of King. "Bill King loved energy and he loved pulling it from your heart. You couldn't not be involved. His photos were athletic, sensual. He'd have a diamond necklace strung from your mouth to someone else's. He'd have you jumping over camera boxes, or part of a chorus line."

When Reno was twenty-three, she gave up the $3,000 cover shots and the European trips and went back home. "I never wanted to be a supermodel, a star. I wanted to make my niche and represent women in a positive light and when I left the business I was frustrated," she explains. "I was not paid for my opinion, that was someone else's job. Basically, my role was to make the outfit or the product look good." Reno attended Miami Community College. She refused modeling work for six months and got a massage therapy license; for the next year and a half she took classes during the week and modeled for European catalog companies on the weekend.

In November 1993, Reno was asked to speak on behalf of her aunt, Attorney General Janet Reno, at a *Glamour* magazine, Woman of the Year Awards Ceremony in New York. The event was attended by 350 women, all achievers in various professions, and it spurred the Miami native to think about returning to her modeling career. Older and wiser this time around, Reno had a focus and a strategy. "I wanted to portray healthy, strong, confident women, or women wanting to discover their strength," she says, "and I wanted to look approachable. Then I looked at the magazines and what kinds of identity matched my personal ideals." Some of the magazines she aimed for were *Mirabella, New Woman, Shape,* and *Self.*

Although Reno had a plan in mind, modeling agencies weren't receptive to her return. Initially, Elite didn't want to represent Reno, even with her track record. "I understand why an agency wouldn't want to take me back," she says candidly. "I was twenty-six years old and it takes time to build a career." She overcame their initial reluctance by meeting with the head of her division and Elite's president, selling them on her strategy and encouraging them to represent women of various ages. It worked. Cover assignments for *Town and Country, New Woman,* and *New York* magazine began pouring in. True to her convictions, the shots are glamorous and appealing or athletic. A *New York* magazine cover catches Reno midair with the Statue of Liberty in the background. She jumped on a trampoline secured to a moving barge for that one.

While Reno has no regrets about her early start, she feels young women should enjoy their teenage years and decide on a career after they turn eighteen. "While the industry is a business, it's very difficult not to become emotionally hurt sometimes because of whether or not people choose to use you," she admits. She credits her family's support and values for helping her stay grounded. "Modeling introduced me to the world," she says gratefully. "It allowed me to get into the nooks and crannies and made me curious."

SHARON COVEY, PATTERN MAKER

Sharon Covey's favorite necklace is a tape measure. It's her constant accessory, whether she's draping and pinning fabric on dress forms or standing over her drafting table creating patterns—patterns that evolve into the knit dresses, tops, pants, shirts, and jackets for women in the Lands' End catalog.

"We have two seasons, fall and winter, and we're developing about fifty new styles for each season. And they are basically all due at the same time," explains Covey in a rare moment of sitting down. "In the beginning of the process—after the designers and merchants put their sketches together, narrowing down about eighty to a hundred ideas, and after the fabrics are selected—I start to drape in my head. Questions like, 'what is the silhouette or the function of the garment? 'Where do you

Sharon Covey, pattern maker

want the neckline?' 'How do you want the garment to fall?' The challenge is keeping track of all the garments, because we gain some, and some drop out."[15]

Covey's official title is team member on the women's knit team for Lands' End, but in actuality, she's the company's head pattern maker/product developer in this area. Her thirteen coworkers include a designer, art director, copywriter, and a merchandiser, so a lot of discussion goes into the development of each piece. "I work with the merchandiser, the manufacturer, and the designer," she says, giving an example. "We may not agree at the same time and will opt for different versions of a style so we can make a final choice later."

Balancing technical know-how with creative interpretation is key for Covey, because it's *her* master plan the clothing manufacturer will follow when it's finally approved. The pattern, a clothing blueprint made on oak tag or marking paper, has specific instructions for details such as size, seams, darts, buttonholes, and gathering. She needs to be able to deal with basic measurements and fractions, to manage a sense of proportion and sizes, to provide clear instructions, and to work well with people.

Every item of clothing on which Covey works may require two or three samples before the final version is agreed on. Lands' End works with about thirty knitwear manufacturers, suppliers who make the clothing, and about 80 percent are United States based. "We try to provide as much information up front to the vendor, so we can both come up with the best garment," Covey said. "Even with our simplest T-shirts. We work with a more tailored fit than most companies, and if we don't provide specific information, we don't get back what we're looking for." Sometimes, Covey meets directly with the vendor. "We usually visit and work with factories on an on-going basis, especially those that are starting up a new line for us," she says. "So, I'm on the road about 25 percent of the time, mostly in the States." Covey also travels to Asia.

A two-week turnaround time, from first pattern to the final version, is the standard for each garment. After the vendor sends back a finished sample based on Covey's measurements and directions, the fit, fabric, style, detail, and sewing quality are ruthlessly scrutinized. The clothing is tried on by a "fit model," someone in a specific size who wears the clothing not for the runway, but to insure the exact fit. Then the garment is put on a "form model," a dummy in a specific size, for further inspection. "You have to have consistent sizing," explains Covey. "Because with us, the customer can't come in and try it on."

For Covey, the rush is on for a four- to five-month period, then there's a lull for a couple of weeks. Covey's twenty-five years in the business have taught her how to have the product ready in time for the tight photo deadlines when the styles are needed, about two months before the catalog comes out. Understanding patterns, grading, markers, fabrics and fabric spreading, manufacturing techniques, and computers are all key to keeping up with the industry, she says.

What attracted her to fashion? An interest in art and drawing kept Covey busy as a young girl. She also sewed, working with basic patterns but changing the details. A two-year associate program at El Centro College in Dallas, which included individual pattern making, drafting, draping, and costume design, helped Covey hone her skills. From there, she worked for various designers and manufacturing companies in Texas, Ohio, North Carolina, New York, and Pennsylvania.

Covey, who says that working with good people and learning from them helped her advance, remembers the advice of one of her college instructors. "She said, 'get your foot in the door, stay alert, and don't act as if you know it all!'"

JACKIE CORSO, MERCHANDISING MANAGER

Some people are lucky. Jackie Corso, vice president and general merchandising manager for Talbots' Hingham, Massachusetts, headquarters, admits to being one of the few. "There's *never* a day when I drive in," said the Boston resident, "that I say, 'Oh God, I have to go to work.'"[16]

Corso has a twenty-year record in retail; sixteen were spent working in department stores including Gimbels in Pittsburgh, the May Company in Connecticut, and Montgomery Ward in Chicago, as assistant buyer, buyer, and division merchandising manager. Before that, Corso studied marketing and retailing at Miami University of Ohio in Oxford, Ohio. Four years ago, she joined Talbots, the specialty chain that *Consumer Reports* rated tops in value and sales help in 1994. Her current assignment is deciding what missy dresses, sportswear, casual clothes, petite apparel, and coats are to be featured on the racks

Jackie Corso, merchandising manager

behind Talbots' red doors, as well as in the pages of its catalogs.

It's a responsibility that might daunt some. The seasonal introductions, four per year developed over three-month periods for the stores and catalog, demand a lot of planning, with different financial strategies for each. As a result, Corso oversees a large team effort. "I go to Europe and shop the fabric and print shows in Florence and Paris and buy samples. The decisions include: Do we buy a new updated version of a color? Do we adapt a trend we see?" explains Corso, who spends an average of three months on the road. That includes two to three European trips, one trip to Asia, and visits to Talbots stores throughout the country to find out what's selling, what isn't, and why.

Corso and her crew look at the trends together, share their ideas, and keep their customers' preferences at the forefront. "We're not designers," she says frankly. "We take what's happening in the fashion industry and translate and modify it for our customers. They may prefer a classic look but they want what's new." Once the swatches of fabrics are culled, the product planning department in Manhattan decides what garments will sell. Then they research their own color and print vendors and develop a color palette. And after that? "We take everyone in our group off-site," explains Corso. "The sweater buyers, the product managers, the casual staff, all go into their own conference room and develop a product. For example, we know there will be X number of sweaters, X number of pants, then we identify the pieces. We devote one whole week to this." After that, the products get designed, and fabrics are sent out to manufacturers for a trial weave or to a color or sketch service in New York.

Then there's the catalog. "The catalog provides us with a lot of information," states Corso. "We can send it out to 300,000 customers and sell 300 pieces, so we use it as a testing vehicle for our store sales. We know if something is a hit within the first ten days of a catalog drop and how many items to project." Corso is already working on the spring catalog, due to appear in five months.

What's a typical day? No such thing, laughs Corso, who clocks in an average ten-hour day, then reads the trade journals after hours. "On a Monday morning, I might look at the previous week's business and check each store by department. I want to look at what business was good, what item really sold so we can react to it, what inventory levels were, if all deliveries were in." Corso has five directors, with responsibilities similar to those of merchandising managers, who report to her. She has two counterparts: a vice president of product development and a vice president of manufacturing.

Styles, shapes, and colors aren't chosen just by Corso and other corporate staff; the customer carries a lot of clout. Prior to the three-month planning sessions, Corso and her group garner feedback from their stores. And they pay attention to customer letters. "We get an incredible amount of customer mail," she says. Talbots' officials have credited their current success to listening to customers, and Corso also cites a workplace that's team-oriented. "It's a very nonretail kind of environment," she says thoughtfully. "No one is yelling and screaming and everyone needs each other. You know you're never going to be out there all alone hanging on a limb."

PATRICIA KANEB, PRESIDENT AND DESIGNER

"I'm unusual," admits Patricia Kaneb thoughtfully. "People look at me differently in the fashion industry because of my business background." Kaneb was sitting in the deep window seat of the final fitting room, a pretty, lilac-pink area with three-way mirrors and chandeliers, big enough to hold a prospective bride and a small army of family and friends.[17]

Kaneb is the new president of Priscilla of Boston, the bridal company that for years has produced beautiful gowns for the rich and famous, including a couple of president's daughters, and many other brides. The company was started nearly fifty years ago by Priscilla Kidder, an industry visionary who shaped each Priscilla bridal dress into a fashion work of art. When Kidder was ready to sell the family business, she handpicked Kaneb as her successor and Kaneb purchased the company in May 1993. Working with a team of five designers, Kaneb is just emerging from her third season, the spring/summer line, a hectic, big market traditionally introduced the first week in October. Kaneb was the creative force behind many of the new gowns—soft clouds of beautiful, ethereal fabrics, some made in tiny Swiss villages. Kaneb admits that her role seesaws between exciting and challenging. "Every six months I ask myself, how am I going to motivate people in another six months," she sighs, thinking about the next big push for April's fall/winter styles.

What sets Kaneb apart is her business background; besides new silhouettes, she designs the future direction of her company. A slender woman of quiet strength, Kaneb spends large chunks of time in her office pouring over profit and loss statements. She reads reports such as the monthly operational statement, a company barometer that tallies the number of gowns sold, what they cost to make, how much time they took to produce, and overall profit. It's this kind of information, as well as an analysis of seasonal and demographic forces, that Kaneb compiles each quarter for bank presentations when she negotiates loans.

Kaneb will be the first to tell you she doesn't do it all. She talks numbers and theories with her financial officer, who produces the company spreadsheet. She talks with her production manager and sets the goals for each month; how many units she needs to get out, how many patterns need to be cut. There are eighty factory work-

Patricia Kaneb, designer and company president

ers—mostly Portuguese-born women, with an average twenty years of service—and a factory in a nearby area. Kaneb is also involved in sales. She communicates goals to her forty retail people, and started giving out cash bonuses to the store managers in 1993.

"You also can't make people feel bad if they don't reach sales goals," she says. "Sometimes things happen they can't control. We moved two stores this year and it wasn't the sales staff's fault that it took customers six months to find the stores. It was hard to see the traffic go down. But it was my decision that made the sales go down and I let the staff know that."

Priscilla is now targeting a different market. While Kaneb honors the quality and service traditions that made Priscilla famous—$30-a-yard fabric, $150-a-yard lace, overall production work by hand—a Priscilla gown is now more affordable. Kaneb made the decision to price the Priscilla line at $1,200 to $1,500 because, "That's where most of the market is." Kaneb also has a couture line, dresses made from custom patterns that range from $3,000 to $9,000 with details like French-stitched seams, silk taffeta linings, and Fortuny-pleated organdy. "I reintroduced something that Priscilla had been known for," says Kaneb, referring admiringly to the founder, Kidder, who still comes in from time to time. "But nowadays only a small part of the population can pay that kind of price."

While the majority of Priscilla customers seek their special dress at one of Kaneb's showrooms, there are 160 wholesale accounts around the country. "I took an existing entity and tweaked things," she says of her managerial approach. It seems to be working; according to Kaneb, a decision to invest $300,000 in advertising in 1994 paid off in a $1.2 million growth in the sales line.

If you think one wedding dress can't be that different from the next, you haven't stood in the crowded showroom aisles, looking at of the company's inventory—about 120 individual gowns. Kaneb explains that thirty to forty new dresses are introduced each season. White is the preferred color for 80 percent of her customers, followed by ivory, but her gowns reflect a variety of lovely hues. Fabric also makes a dress unique. "One of the dresses we've done really well with is our linen dress," she says, pulling out a gown with light embroidery. "It's a fine linen, not the type you think of as bridal," she says, explaining that its popularity rose during the last couple of years as low-key, outdoor weddings became popular. A new addition and major departure for the company was a sheath dress, introduced by Kaneb, a slim, simple floor-length column with a removable train. "Other stores were selling them," she says, "which meant that customers wanted them."

Ideas come to Kaneb in different ways. Sometimes it's a new fabric or lace that sparks inspiration. Sometimes it's a fabric Kaneb sees in a store, or a magazine. "Textures get me going," she says. "I'll see something that I think will translate well into bridal." Her best design thoughts come weekends at her suburban home. "I have to shut down on the weekend," she says. "There are times when I have to sit still and think of nothing and that's when the ideas come." As soon as an idea strikes, Kaneb grabs a pad and pen and writes or sketches. "If I don't write them down as they come, those ideas lose their life," she comments. At a display in her showroom, Kaneb picks up the skirt of a silk organdy gown and points to the delicate, hand-painted flowers above the hem, an idea sparked by a pair of sheer, hand-painted Ungarro palazzo pants she had seen in a magazine.

Kaneb's fashion path began with art and business. As a young girl, Kaneb always sketched; she took art classes through high school. She also remembers playing with the adding machines in her father's office. "My mother had four of us in a row," she says. "And when she needed a break, my father would take us to work." Work was Northeast Petroleum, a regional heating oil and gas distributor. The company, started by her grandfather who was the son of Lebanese immigrants, was run by her father and uncle, and Kaneb worked in Northeast's credit office during high school summers. "My mother came from very humble beginnings," she says. "She was always busy and industrious and we were all encouraged to have summer jobs."

Kaneb wasn't sorry she chose liberal arts courses with a major in English and history at Cornell University. "It's the only time in your life you ever take courses like these; they influence the way you look at the world and help you learn reasoning skills," she says. Her career path included a stint as manager of the accessories department for a Filene's Department store outside of Boston, a job that didn't go as well as Kaneb had hoped.

Kaneb checked inventory, stocked, and managed a workforce of part-time women who had worked in that department for years. "It was easy to recognize they knew more than I did," she says candidly. "And I felt I had no reason to be manager of these people. I couldn't earn their respect. The learning curve was too steep." After a year, Kaneb wanted more business experience and earned an M.B.A. at Boston University, worked as a fund accountant at Fidelity, and as a commercial loan officer at Baybank.[18] "I was disappointed when the retailing position at Filene's didn't work out," she admits. "I felt like I was bouncing around, but when I look back, it all made sense. I learned a lot. I did a lot of financial analysis and big picture stuff and learned the ins and outs of big companies."

She was brought together with Priscilla Kidder by a college friend who interned and worked for the former owner. When Kidder began looking for a buyer, the friend suggested Kaneb call her. Kaneb did, extending an invitation for lunch at the elegant Ritz Hotel. "We really clicked," Kaneb recalls. "I loved design and had a understanding of family businesses from my time as a commercial loan officer. And she had built her business over the last forty years and wanted to sell her company to a woman. Remember, she was one of the few female heads of a major company in her day, a kind of Vera Wang of her time." Kaneb used trust fund money, set up when her father and uncle sold Northeast in 1983, as capital to buy Priscilla. The match was the culmination of a dream, but the idea of selling bridal gowns was especially appealing because "you're not forcing something the customer doesn't want."

Still, she is concerned about her future labor force,

A Priscilla of Boston employee rushes finished gowns
from workroom to showroom.

although Kaneb says she pays $10 to $12 an hour and
provides health coverage. "The women really care about
their work and feel the finished product has them in it,"
she says admiringly. "But their kids don't want to do it
and I really worry about the labor force drying up. It's still
working well now though—because some employees have

relatives who come to this country, so they bring in a niece or a cousin looking for work."

MARYANN PUGLISI, AGENCY BOOKER

Maryann Puglisi's workplace is an energy-charged environment. Models, photographers, and walk-in hopefuls are always in the background, and the conversations, including those of her coworkers, swirl around the large, black circular table she shares with six other bookers. "We're separated like pieces in a pie and my computer is at the central point," Puglisi explains, bridging her hands in a triangle for emphasis. "There's always traffic here and I have to block out the noise and speak up on the phone if I want to be heard." Sometimes, Puglisi admits with a laugh, it's hard to shake the effects. "When I get home, my husband tells me, 'what are you hollering at? I'm right here.'"[19]

Puglisi represents twenty-five young women in the Model Management Division of Elite in New York, one of the top modeling agencies in the country, founded and still run by John Casablancas. While getting the best modeling jobs for these young women is the major focus, her efforts don't stop when the deal is made. "I'm like a mother," she says. "I tell them, 'Make sure you have this and this. Call me when you get there. Let me know if there are any problems.' I have access to a travel agent and if someone is stuck at an airport, I can get her home. They know they can call on weekends or at three in the morning if they need me."

What exactly does a booker do? "When I come in, all the faxes are here from Europe," she says of her half-past nine starting time. "They say, 'yes, I have a job for you,' or 'I'm working on one,' or 'I have something tentative.' I also check a pad for the list of models who weren't reached the night before about potential jobs. I make calls

Maryann Puglisi, agency booker

to Europe. I clear up any tentative bookings; it's not good for the model if you haven't gotten an okay in two weeks." Then Puglisi works to get details from clients about future assignments, such as whether the shoot will feature lingerie as well as fashion. "Some models don't want to do see-through or lingerie. For some jobs, models have to be lingerie-ready and swimwear-ready." The clients pay the travel costs and make the arrangements. "They pay for airfare, hotel, and expenses," Puglisi explains. And for travel time if a model must travel during business hours. While Puglisi represents twenty-five models, she doesn't need to check in with each of them daily; still, most days she juggles calls to and from twelve to fifteen of these women, who use portable phones and beepers.

Just about all her bookings come from magazine, catalog, and product ad clients. Puglisi will set up a "go see," where the model goes to see a client; other times she'll forward "books" (collections of earlier ads and photos) on several models for a job such as a jewelry advertisement. To move things along, Puglisi uses a personal approach and sets up dinners with clients a couple of times a week. "I like meeting people and having that contact," she explains. "I don't have to hound the client. I can sit and show books, which have everything a model's done, and say, 'this one is really great,' 'this one would be really good for you.'" But she also dines with her models to keep abreast of what's going on in their lives or to celebrate their successes. A constant upbeat approach, which Puglisi warmly radiates, is vital. Without it, she says, "you can't project enthusiasm to your clients."

Four times a week, Puglisi wrests herself away from her headset and meets with walk-in interviewees, young hopefuls who want to break into the business. She also sees prospects referred by scouts or modeling schools, and looks over mail-ins. Personality is just as important as physical appearance, she says. "Clients are looking for movement, warmth, a smile. If a girl is beautiful, but a drip, they may not book her." What the young woman projects is important because she's the one who sells the clothes or the product, Puglisi feels. "With Iman," she says, naming a current celebrity model as an example, "no matter what you put on her, she's a diva on the runway. It has to do with the model, not what she's wearing.

You can have a model in a cheap polyester dress who makes it look like a Saks evening dress."

There are three main Elite divisions: New Faces, a training area for newcomers; Model Management, Puglisi's area, which focuses on building a model's career; and Elite, which handles the superstars of the industry, like Linda Evangelista. "It's not a short-term career," says Puglisi. "A woman can go way past thirty. You can find them as young as thirteen to fourteen years old and some have really good potential. By the time they are twenty-nine, thirty, thirty-one, they can be well established with steady clients."

The models Puglisi represents, including Hunter Reno, start at a daily rate of $1,250, for catalog work with such clients as Bloomingdale's, Saks Fifth Avenue, and Spiegel. The rate can jump to $4,000 to $5,000 a day, depending on the model, but the work isn't as easy as it looks, points out Puglisi. "Who wants to pose for an hour at a time under hot lights?" she asks. "You have to put up with people touching you all the time, arranging your clothing, your hair. If you're used to doing your makeup one way, someone does it differently. The days can be long. Sometimes you have to go from trip to trip. I would like the model to be able to go home and refresh herself, but if there's work, you've got to go."

Puglisi, who was born and raised in the Bronx, New York, has been a booker for sixteen years, most of that time at Elite. "There are no set rules," she says about her position. "You learn on the job as the years go on. I've had my flubs. When I first started out I called and asked to speak to Ann Klein and the person on the other end of the phone said, 'Ann Klein has been dead for three years.' You have to pick and choose which areas you feel would be best for your model and advise her. Out of two magazines, maybe this one isn't that great, but it has excellent photography. Her life and career depend on the agency and how we think and operate."

DENNITA SEWELL, COLLECTIONS MANAGER AT THE COSTUME INSTITUTE, METROPOLITAN MUSEUM OF ART

Dennita Sewell is a keeper of the flame for fashions past. When she starts her day and unlocks the door to the storage room of the Costume Institute, there's a little jump in her stomach, a mixture of awe and excitement about what the day might bring. Handling a new acquisition for the first time, perhaps sixteenth-century doublets (close-fitting men's jackets), may be part of the agenda. Or, to help a fashion student, she may open a drawer and carefully unfold one of her favorite garments—James Galanos's exquisite "Aurora Borealis" creation, a gold lamé couture gown from the 1950s with a strapless bodice covered with crystals that dazzle and burst with color and light.[20]

As collections manager at the Costume Institute of the Metropolitan Museum of Art in New York City, Sewell is the key figure in coordinating what students and designers are looking for with the holdings of the institute. She also oversees the storage of the collection, which consists of 70,000 objects—clothing and accessories, mostly from Europe and the Western Hemisphere. It includes an amazing range of objects. Some are very rare, such as a pair of medieval shoes, sixteenth-century doublets, and a 1690s mantua (a columnlike garment that is one of the earliest dresses in American fashion history), and garments from the eighteenth century. Clothing from the nineteenth and twentieth centuries include garments from the great French couture houses such as Worth, Chanel, and Dior, as well as some by innovative, brilliant American talents like Claire McCardell. In addition, there are regional collections from everywhere in the world, including sumptuous velvet garments with gold brocade from India, and intricate and beautifully patterned African hats of beads and shells.

Dennita Sewell, collections manager at the Costume
Institute, Metropolitan Museum of Art

The Institute presents exhibitions built around a
theme—such as the popular 1996 "Haute Couture"
exhibit—that are open to the public. Most of the people
who come to study the collection are either fashion stu-

dents, theater students, or designers, who book appointments with Sewell about two weeks in advance. They may ask for clothing by specific designers, or their need may be for a certain style, or for period garments. Sewell makes the selection and has the clothing ready at the appointment time, then answers questions, points out a garment's unique features, and suggests other items if something else is needed. Requests vary from the scholarly to the unusual. "Last week I had a performance artist call," she says, shaking her head in amazement. "He was doing something with a bullfighting scene and wanted to know the weight of a toreador's cape." About 350 people a year use the resources at the institute, including student classes from Parsons, the Fashion Institute of Technology, and Pratt Institute.

Who are the designers who use the collection? Vivienne Westwood, a London designer, for one, says Sewell. Westwood, a feisty, avant-garde woman who helped start the punk fashion movement in Britain in the early 1970s, has talked about her visits to museums for ideas and once commented, "this is the only century that hasn't had respect for the past."[21]

"Vivienne believes in looking at historical pieces for inspiration," explains Sewell. "She feels it's the way to keep from drying up as a designer, that it can't all possibly come from you. She looks at Worth, Dior, Balenciaga. She reviews construction techniques, the way things are made and cut, and has her assistants sometimes sketch or measure parts of the garment to see its proportions." Sewell recognized the usefulness of research when she saw Westwood's fall 1994 Paris show. It included bustled evening dresses in beautiful silk satin, reminiscent of the late nineteenth century. Sewell was in Europe on a grant to study the storage areas and techniques of costume collections in England, Germany, and France.

Among the rows and rows of fashions at the Costume Institute she must have a favorite or two. "Oh," she says, hesitantly, "it's impossible to say." When prompted, she talks about the mantua, with its Elizabethan bodice embroidered with vegetables and flowers; the riveting James Galanos "Aurora Borealis" gown that she first saw as an intern; and the Venus and Junon dresses from Christian Dior's 1949 collection, with their layers of silk net, huge skirts, yards and yards of fabric, and sequined, embroidered petal shapes in subtle color combinations of pale to dark gray—explosions of postwar fashion celebration after fabric restrictions were lifted. Dior, Balenciaga, and McCardell are the most asked-for designers, she says.

During a tour of the storage rooms, Sewell points to some nineteenth-century capes in cupboardlike compartments. "These woolen things can hang easily." The storage compartments are situated back-to-back in wide aisles and there are several rooms full, all temperature-controlled at sixty-five degrees Farenheit, 50 percent humidity. "But this silk-satin Worth dress," she adds, pulling out a deep bottom drawer, "has a separate bodice, and it's more delicate, so it has to be stored in a drawer." The fashions all have labels sewn into them with an assigned museum number. An additional, visible tag offers information about the piece, the donor, and a number. Sewell is reorganizing the twentieth-century section, which has been chronological, so that the garments will be grouped by designer instead. About two days a week are devoted to the institute's storage. The rest of her time is devoted to appointments and working with the curator of the collection on exhibitions; there are three a year.

New York's Metropolitan Museum of Art is a long way from Hale, Missouri, a small farming community of 480 people in the northwestern part of the state. Sewell lived on a 400-acre farm and learned to sew before she could read, helping her mother and grandmother with the quilts they made. "My family has lived in this area since the early 1800s. My dad raises soybeans and we had a dairy farm for a while," she explains. "Going to college wasn't the expected thing to do, but I was valedictorian in my high school and got a full scholarship to the University of Missouri."

Sewell, who signed up for a work-study program, didn't initially know what to enroll in. When she walked in on a campus theater production something clicked. "They were getting ready to design and execute the play, and Janet Arnold's book *Patterns of Fashions* was laid out on a long table. I saw its diagrams of period costumes and very precise notes and I was hooked." Sewell signed up for a program in textile and apparel management. Next came an internship in New York with The Costume Collection, a nonprofit group that rents costumes to not-for-profit theaters and shows, and a student textile-study tour of Europe. Between college and graduate school, Sewell served a six-month stint as dressmaker for Bermans and Nathans, a London shop that produces costumes for plays and film. Graduate work in design at Yale's School of Drama followed, in an intense three-year program.

After graduation, Sewell was stitching tote bags at a factory in New Haven, a job she'd held while at Yale, trying to decide what her next step would be when her mentor and teacher from The Costume Collection, Whitney Blausem, called to tell her about a position at the museum. "She said, 'I know it's not design, but....'" recalls Sewell. "I listened to her because she's been the most influential figure in my life, encouraging me about the internship, and to go for my master's at Yale. So I have a certain level of trust when Whitney calls. I really wanted the job, but I didn't want to get too hopeful and I remember thinking when I went to the interview, 'even if I don't get the position, at least I had a day at the Met.'" Sewell got more than a day; she was hired for the job in 1993.

Since then, Janet Arnold, the scholar and authority on costume design whose book so influenced Sewell, has researched at the institute and sent Sewell a note of thanks. What constantly amazes Sewell is meeting the people she's admired over the years. "I look at things I've clipped out for my scrapbook, like Vivienne Westwood's fashions when I worked in London. Now," she says with a touch of awe, "I know these people."

ZELDA WYNN, COSTUME DESIGNER, DANCE THEATRE OF HARLEM

"What was the most memorable gown you ever made?" Zelda Wynn was asked. Wynn sifted through a mental record of images from the years when she designed beautiful, distinctive gowns for singer Ella Fitzgerald, performer Josephine Baker, opera great Jessye Norman, movie star Marlene Dietrich, pop singer Gladys Knight, and many other celebrities. Then there were also the gowns she custom-made for the women who flocked to her dress shop, Zelda Modiste, on 158th Street and Broadway in New York City, where chauffeured limosines waited outside, lined up in a row. Later, in the 1950s, the shop was moved downtown to a location near Carnegie Hall and renamed Chez Zelda.

"I made a dress for Joyce Bright, a great singer who performed all over the United States and Europe. The dress was so tight, they had to carry her onto the stage," Wynn remembers. "She was photographed in it for *Life* magazine."[22] It was called a trumpet gown, hugging the body to the knees and then cascading to the floor in ruffles. The gown was heavy with silver bugle beads sewn on pale pink silk.

Zelda Wynn has designed and sewn hundreds, or perhaps thousands of gowns and costumes—first for celebrities and private clients, more recently for New York's acclaimed Dance Theatre of Harlem. In 1969 Wynn, then sixty-four, joined the new dance company as costume designer and sewing instructor. She created and made their costumes and traveled with the company to theaters in the United States and in twenty foreign countries. When the dancers were on stage, Wynn stood in the wings and watched, alongside Arthur Mitchell, the Dance Theatre's founder and artistic director. "My boss would stand right beside me, always telling me that something should be made longer, or shorter, or tighter," Wynn laughs.

Wynn stopped making costumes five years ago, but she still conducts design and sewing classes and maintains the wardrobe for the company's dance school. Five days a week, from 8:30 A.M. to 4:30 P.M., she can be found in the dance company's school wardrobe room, a brightly lit space with shelves crammed full of tap shoes, ballet slippers, and other dance staples, and dominated by a long measuring table. Besides conducting classes here, she repairs costumes, helps students find specific items, and works with teachers who need changes in a costume. This morning, Wynn was expecting a dance teacher who was coming to make eight tutus.

Wynn's first designs were for dolls' clothing, which she began creating as a three-year-old in Chambersburg, Pennsylvania. She was the oldest of seven children, and her mother taught her to sew. In high school, she made clothing for herself and her grandmother—clothing that stood out for its fine detail and craftsmanship.

Later, Flossie Hawkins, the wife of Erskine Hawkins who was a famous black trumpet player and band leader, introduced Wynn to Ella Fitzgerald. Fitzgerald was beginning her singing career and needed a gown. "She only came one time to be fitted," Wynn remembers. "After that, she refused to be fitted,"—even though her weight would increase along with her fame. Whenever she needed a gown, she contacted Wynn who studied photographs to guess the performer's size. The arrangement worked. "She would tell me, 'everything you make fits me.'" says Wynn.

Zelda Wynn, costume designer, in the wardrobe room
at the Dance Theatre of Harlem

"This was my first dress shop," Wynn says as she shows a small 1940s black-and-white photo of Zelda Modiste. The attractive store, with hats and accessories in the window, was decorated by Wynn. "I was the first black to have a business on Broadway," she says. The staff included one saleswoman and nine dressmakers who sewed everything to order. While a customer was being measured, Wynn sketched a style and showed it for approval. The best materials were used, and Wynn would get tips on fabrics from garment manufacturers who had business nearby and took evening strolls past the

Broadway stores. "They would pass my shop and come in and recommend places where I could get certain fabrics," Wynn remembers. Workdays were long. "Most times, I worked six days and six nights. I had a deadline on everything I made so I worked very hard," she says. She also gave sewing classes, teaching her skills to other women.

How did Wynn connect with the Dance Theatre? "Zelda was training young people to sew in a special program and my nieces were taking her class," recalls Arthur Mitchell, the founder of the company. In 1955 Mitchell was the first African-American male dancer to become a permanent member of a major ballet company, The New York City Ballet. Later, he set out to create a dance program for Harlem children. The Dance Theatre was founded in 1969 and is well known for its dance company and its school of allied arts. "I said, 'I want that woman who taught my nieces to sew,'" Mitchell explains. Wynn was hired to design and teach; the students made the costumes under her instruction.

It's one thing to design styles for celebrities and wealthy clients. It's another to interpret the costumes for dance. Dancers express magic, whimsy, drama, anger, joy, and passion through the energy of their bodies. To convey these expressions through costume is a major accomplishment. Mitchell agrees. "Zelda has strict discipline and remembers everything. What is incredible is that she was able to carry her design and technique from fashion to costume. That doesn't happen often," he says.

Wynn is modest about her achievements and says that the design ideas just came. She watched the dance company rehearse and then worked to capture the essence of their dance. "I sketched designs," she says, "and showed them to the choreographer. Some choreographers, like Geoffrey Holder, brought their own sketches. His were so beautifully done that they were easy to interpret." At times, the company's work meant that she had to work five days and five nights straight to complete costumes for a performance. Once her assignment included refurbishing 3,000 red-velvet seats at the Loew's Theater on 125th Street—a task that was captured in a treasured photograph of Wynn sitting amid stacks of fabric. "There were 12,000 pieces of velvet," Mitchell remembers.

A photo collage from 1969 shows Zelda Wynn facing the challenge of recovering 3,000 theater seats.

"Every seat needed four pieces, and she covered every seat in the house for our first homecoming gala."[23]

Some of Wynn's masterpieces are recorded in two large scrapbooks. From the "Kennedy Center Tonight" performance of Stravinsky's ballet "Firebird," Wynn points out the firebird's striking headpiece and dress, with strips of red, yellow, and purple feathers, tulle, and other material. For a production of "Fête Noir," she designed sharp military jackets—a style she had never done before.

Andrea Ross, head of wardrobe for the CBS television network, remembers working with Wynn in the 1970s at the dance company. "Wynn comes from the heart. She always dealt with things as a mother and was concerned with everything. If something could be done better, she made you make it better. She taught me that no matter where you are in life, you don't have to settle. It helped me a lot."[24]

LYDIA CAFFERY, CREATIVE DIRECTOR

If you think denims are standard fabrics with little variation, Lydia Caffery creative director of Avondale Mills will set you straight. "We run about forty-five different versions of denim," she explains in her office at Avondale Mills in Sylacauga, Alabama. "The yarn is dyed in indigo, what we call range-dyed indigo, and goes through a lengthy process. It's dipped eight times, which creates a ring-dyed effect with the indigo colors heaviest at the outside, and lightest on the inside."[25]

Then the fabrics go through a shading process. "The more you wash it, the more the indigo comes off," Caffery continues. "You can wash it with stone or chemicals, which causes a bleached effect. Or you can combine the processes." Weights of the fabric differ, too, she points out. "The consistency can range from fine, with high-density level threads, to a more coarse fabric, with a lower

Lydia Caffery, creative director

level of density. Or you can have left-hand twill, or the more typical, right-hand twill, or herringbone or poplin."

Caffery is creative director for Avondale Mills, a hundred-year-old fabric mill in Alabama, where she heads the design and marketing efforts. Avondale's leading product is denim, but it also produces yarn-dyed plaids, stripes, and patterns in a heavyweight cotton. Four fabric stylists report to Caffery, and a big part of her job is forecasting what the consumer will want in two years. "We're responsible for helping Lee fabricate its denim line," she says, citing their biggest customer; the Gap is also a client. "That means we have to provide the right fabrics." To do this, Caffery writes trend analyses and reports to educate her clients about what she sees. "Right now there's a return to dark indigo denim, it's just starting to happen," she says. Caffery photographs consumers wearing dark indigo denim and shows the slides to clients so they can see the new wave of consumer preference as it swells, note which cities the trend has hit, and which consumers are responding.

Fashion forecasting entails about 75 percent travel time in the United States and Europe. "I shop stores," she says. "I talk to a lot of companies, manufacturers, buyers, and journalists in the business. Presentations are made twice a year to the customer," she explains. "The research is a full six-month project. We start in July, for example, to project a color two years out. In August, we begin researching the fabric trends. We make final choices in November and present them to the client in December." When a decision is made on a fabric, it is produced at the Alabama mill and yarn-dyed. Caffrey reviews the sample and makes sure it passes the quality test before a run is made. And there's a lot of contact with the customer. Design standards, quality, and how to produce what the customer wants at the right price points are all judgement calls she has to make and negotiate.

It's Caffery's job to be enthusiastic about her company's fabric, and she is, presenting it as America's trademark fabric. "In a cultural sense, it is," agrees Bill Daddy, director of public relations for Cotton Incorporated, a research and promotion company for the cotton industry. Denim became the style and fabric for youth in the 1950s, he says. "Prior to that, there was more formality in dress and this interesting glamour; but the sobering experiences of the Depression and World War II led the country to reexamine its values. In the 1960s when polyester came out, the group from the 1950s who were so accustomed to cotton T-shirts and denim jeans and the way they felt, never gave them up and their kids adopted the look. Denim got its first boost into high fashion with designer jeans in the 1970s." While we think of it as an American fabric, denim's origins are European, says Daddy. "It began in Genoa, Italy, or De Nimes, France, we're not sure which. Levi Strauss was an Eastern European immigrant who saw the fabric's potential and his product became the uniform of the West."[26]

Caffery, a New Orleans transplant who now resides in Birmingham, Alabama, designed her own clothes in high school. After graduation from the Tobé Coburn School and Parsons School of Design in New York, she started out in the business as a salesperson for Ann Taylor, a retail chain, in 1980. "Retail is the most difficult part of the business, but it's also the most vital," she says. "If you can understand retail, you can understand anything." Later, she worked as an associate fashion director for Macy's in New York, led the creative effort at Cotton Incorporated, worked in public relations and for a fashion forecasting company, and was editor of the *Tobé Report*, a long-established forecasting service.

While Caffery goes to an occasional fashion show, she's more interested in watching what people are wearing in the streets and stores. Why? "The clothing may be fantastic on the runway," she says practically. "But that's not necessarily what the consumer wants."

YVETTE FRY, PRESIDENT, ACCESSORIES COMPANY

"There I was, a puppy from El Paso, meeting Calvin Klein," recalls Yvette Fry, president of Yvette Fry, Inc., an upper-end fashion accessories company. The meeting took place about 1980 when Fry worked for a small upstart jewelry company that designed hand-carved ebony and exotic wood pieces. Fry acted as the sales representative, answered the phones, packed boxes, and called fashion editors. "At the time, we were the only company that specialized in exotic wood and Calvin needed the accessories for a runway show. That's when Calvin was at the absolute top. I was petrified before I went in. But he was very nice, very professional. But that's why he became what he is," says Fry admiringly, "because of his professionalism."[27]

Professionalism, Fry will tell you, is a powerful business attribute, one that she constantly seeks to cultivate. Fashion icons such as Calvin Klein reinforced its importance when she met him as she was just starting out. And before that—when she was a fashion student at the Tobé Coburn school, which offers marketing, merchandising, and management programs in fashion—professionalism, and concern about how you presented yourself were drilled in daily. "That's why I'm still in business," she says, surrounded by dozens of attractively arranged displays in her Fifth Avenue showroom. Fry went out on her own in 1986; her first showroom was a twenty-by-thirty foot space where she was the sole employee with two phone lines. Now Fry has seven lines constantly ringing, and eight employees. About thirty-five designers supply her with accessories. Three thousand accounts, including department stores such as Saks Fifth Avenue, Nieman Marcus, and Macy's, and Robert Redford's Sundance catalog, buy them, says Fry.

Fry started in El Paso, where she was born and raised, an only child in a middle-class household where both parents worked. Her father had a job in the accounting department of El Paso Natural Gas; her mother was head operator of the local telephone company. Fry remembers pouring over fashion magazines and making her own jewelry in high school. Who was her first role model? "Mom was into fashion. So I guess I got it from her. She was voted best dressed in El Paso in the 1950s when the newspapers reported what you wore and the type of canapés

Yvette Fry, accessories company president

you served at a party," Fry explains, chuckling with affection. Jeans and cowboy boots were Fry's fashion basics in high school, but accessories became a passion and she began making her own jewelry. "I was always into accessories because it was the cheapest way to change your look," she says.

Fry began her career after high school. "I remember seeing ads for various fashion schools in the back of magazines that said, 'spend a week in New York.' Well I decided I should be in New York *all* the time. So a counselor looked into schools for me." Fry managed an interview with a Tobé Coburn representative at Nieman Marcus in Dallas. "I was very nervous. I wore my own jewelry and remember the interviewer commenting on it, probably because it was so ugly," she laughs. "But at least I was accessorized."

Fry, who for the most part had never been outside her Texas hometown, was accepted and made the move to New York. "Tobé Coburn was a spectacular school then," Fry says. "It was very disciplined. You couldn't wear open-toe shoes, because if you got your toes soiled, it didn't look professional. The original hat racks were still there from the times students wore hats and gloves. We hated the rules, but they taught us discipline and professionalism. That's key. The main thing in business is to follow up and follow through. I never want a customer to complain. I tell my staff, 'If you don't have an answer for a customer, tell them you'll get back to them. Then do it.'"

After graduation, Fry looked up the jewelry and accessory companies listed in *Vogue* and *Harper's Bazaar* and sent them her résumé. Besides Calvin Klein, Fry remembers supplying accessories to Donna Karan and Louis Dell'Olio when they were designers for Anne Klein. "We were lucky," she says. "The accessories business is small and fashion editors were familiar with the line. Designers would call the magazines asking, 'do you know someone who has this look?' The editors would tell them about our jewelry and the designers would contact us."

Over a six-year period, Fry worked with three different jewelry accessory companies. Then she struck out on her own. "It was the only way there was any growth potential," she says. "How long can you get by on $18,000 a year, if I was even making that much?" She put $4,000 into her business: $2,000 from her savings and $2,000 from her parents who told her to go for it.

"I was living on my own in a tiny studio apartment in Hoboken, New Jersey, and decided I would sink or swim. I was never that worried," says Fry candidly. "I was worried before I opened the showroom but my feeling was, 'this is what I want, this is what I know.'" Fry had contacts with fashion editors; she also knew jewelry and accessory manufacturers. What was needed were designers she could represent and buyers who wanted to purchase their lines. After eight months of cold calls, Fry accumulated twenty designers. Then she sent out a newsletter describing her merchandise and their prices to buyers all over the country. It was printed on can't miss fuchsia paper. "I didn't want it to get lost," says Fry, smiling. "I knew it worked when buyers came to the showroom and I'd see the newsletter peeking out of their briefcases."

After three expansions, Fry doesn't have to make cold calls anymore. A tiny back office, separated by a curtain, hums with staff answering phones. "I have an excellent staff," said Fry, who insists hiring good people is essential. In the morning, her employees follow up on fax orders from the retailers, the department and specialty stores, and catalog companies, as well answer questions from designers and manufacturers. The rest of the day, customers are contacted for reorders. "That's why you have to be organized," she says. "The phones are ringing all day, thank goodness." Pressure builds during market week, five intense buying periods during the first weeks of January, March, May, August, and November. Fry's staff contacts buyers three weeks before to book showroom appointments for them. In addition, there's a fashion accessory show three times a year. Fry displays ten to twelve of her lines in booths at the show.

While her staff works on follow-up, Fry concentrates on working with designers on the newest trends. "Banana Republic might come in and need a belt with a brown buckle," she explains as an example. "I'll go to one of my designers and help them work it out. I have to be creative and I have to rein in creative people so that their end result is salable. I also look for new designers to represent. I check out the mark-down counters to see what isn't selling in stores. And I travel to different cities to see what's out there." For trend research, Fry scouts New York and Los Angeles shops. She also scans *Women's Wear Daily* and forecasting reports and uses buying services that shop for accessories from Europe.

Is a designer's work harder than what Fry does? "It's difficult to be a designer," Fry says thoughtfully. "But I think what I do is more complicated. I'm dealing with designers *and* retailers. If a shipment doesn't come in, it reflects on me." She also has to take a risk when going with unknowns. Fry walks over to an assortment of fabric-covered hair accessories. "I've done $1 million of sales on these," she says. "When the designers first came to me, they brought their product in a cardboard box and were pretty inexperienced. You have to trust your instinct that a line is good enough to do. Sometimes the product comes before the trend. Sometimes the trend comes before the product."[28]

Merchandising her designers' accessories in the showroom requires a balance of artistry and sales ability, something she learned during an internship at Saks Fifth Avenue. "I worked with a terrific woman named Jane Tuma who taught me how to make the merchandise speak for itself. Little points, such as placing things straight, not diagonally, not having a display too cluttered or too open."

Handbags, belts, hats, jewelry, hair accessories, shawls, and home items, with their designers' names framed in silver, neatly line Fry's neutral-colored walls. "You can put up stuff," says Fry, standing in front of a line called Collezione, "but if it doesn't have a story, it doesn't work. You have to make the buyer focus." She indicates the five shelves of Collezione belts, bags, and hats. "People typically look from left to right," she says. Fry points out the groupings by material: rayon braid, boucle, and chenille, and by color that ranges from light to dark. One shelf had a taupe-hued grouping; another ranged from soft purple to teal.

"I always move things around so that it looks fresh," Fry says, adding that a good display area never remains static.

LAURA DUNN, SENIOR BUYER

Christmas was only seven months away. And Laura Dunn didn't want to display the same old red bras. "I always believed inner wear worn as outer wear could work," explains Dunn, senior buyer for Burdines' intimate apparel. "There had to be something different."

Dunn had vacationed in California the summer before and found a glimpse of what could be. "I saw leather bustiers in some of the funky stores and it triggered something," she remembers. Back home, the bustier idea stayed with her. Dunn kept seeing them in magazines she browsed through. Then a California-based company that manufactured bustiers called. The owner had a New York showroom, and Dunn met with her during a business trip. The merchandise was beautiful, but too expensive for Dunn. "But when I left the showroom, I peeked in another showroom in the same building," she says. The manufacturer produced some private label lines and had what Dunn wanted at the right price.

"We worked on color and style," said Dunn. "We came up with one bustier that had multiple hooks, another had a halter top, one looked like a swimsuit. They had sequins, crystals, and velvet. It was a lot of fun and I set the trend for holiday glitz on the floor."[29] The bustiers, priced from $30 to $90, were introduced in October 1991 for the holiday season and sold wildly in the Burdines'

Laura Dunn, senior buyer

stores. "They did $200,000—that was for a seasonal business in a ten-week period," says Dunn with pride.

Taking a gamble, is part of her job. "You're a risk taker," says Dunn, ticking off the elements it takes to be a successful buyer. "It means having the right merchandise at the right time at the right price." As a senior buyer of Burdines' Miami flagship store, Dunn is responsible for the 200 to 300 items a season that are displayed on the intimate apparel floor, their sizes, and styles. How does she accomplish this for thirty-eight stores? "Burdines has a planning organization but we provide direction. For example, we decide on the assortment of intimate apparel items, and the ten stores where they should be placed. The planning organization tells us 'this is what it will cost you.' When they get the green light from us, they distribute them."

Dunn is enthusiastic about her job and seems relaxed despite an upcoming business trip to New York. "I don't travel as much as people in ready-wear, but I do take eight to nine trips a year to New York and I try to visit ten of our stores within a six-month period. Otherwise, I'm glued to my desk 80 percent of the time," she says.

What happens at Dunn's desk isn't boring. Her day is crammed with decisions that involve financial analysis, trend awareness, people skills, collaboration, delegation, and problem solving. "The first thing I do in the morning is compare sales from the day before with the plan I have, which is determined six months in advance. I look at whether we are running a strong promotion. If I'm meeting the sales plan or beating it. I evaluate it." A senior associate buyer reports to Dunn. She also works with two planners who set up the apparel in the stores and determine the color, style, and sizes. "We all sit together daily and talk about current sales."

Twelve major vendors supply Dunn's stores. "I can spend a full day on back-to-back appointments with sales representatives," she says. She meets with her reps to discuss the success of a line, upcoming advertising, and how to plan for a new item. National and regional division managers touch base every eight weeks at the Miami store; sometimes they hold strategy meetings. "The stores are automated, so you have to make time to check out that systems," she adds. "That means scanning the pricing from the cash registers to make sure it's correct, checking that we're getting the right credit for a sale." In addition, her everyday schedule has to include internal meetings, and time to write merchandise orders.

Dunn says no crystal ball exists to predict the next fashion trend; she uses more reliable techniques. She evaluates the competition. A liaison visits stores outside the chain every six weeks, and brings in whatever is new that Burdines doesn't have. Dunn studies *Women's Wear Daily* and *BFIA,* an intimate apparel trade publication. South Beach, a hot section in Miami that runs along Ocean Drive is a place to find new trends. "It's very hip," says Dunn. "There are boutiques, modeling agencies, and art deco hotels. A lot of model photo shoots are done here, including French and German ones, so you get a sense of what Europeans are wearing."[30]

Burdines is part of the Federated retail chain, and four times a year Dunn flies to New York to participate in a team project called market week, during which events are held with vendors for the entire Federated chain, which includes Macy's and Stern's stores. A lot of wheeling and dealing on sales is done there. Dunn gives an example. "We'll say to a vendor, 'what quantities do you need us to order so we can be first in the market?'" That takes place the first week. The week after market week, she meets with vendors on an individual basis, solely for Burdines.

Who chooses the laces and fabrics that change the look of intimate apparel? "The styling direction comes from European trends. Our corporate people go to Germany and France and meet with the small manufacturers, the lace, satin, and bow people. We have a product development area that gives us color direction, which we then give to the manufacturers."

Interestingly, Dunn didn't start out planning for a

fashion career. She worked part-time during high school selling candy and stationery at Jordan Marsh in Miami, and loved retailing. "It was those Godiva samples," she says laughing. "I loved talking to people and had good managers who saw my potential. As time passed, when my manager went away on vacation, she put me in charge of scheduling and I liked the responsibility."

Part-time work was one thing; a career was another. Dunn didn't want to work in sales as a long-term commitment. Health care seemed attractive. But the required three semesters of physics changed her mind about nursing. So Dunn concentrated on what she loved and what she was good at—retail sales and numbers—and took marketing courses at the University of Florida in Gainesville. "Around the time I graduated, in 1982, you could choose finance or merchandising as a career path in retail. I figured that if I didn't like merchandising, I could go into operations, which involved finance," she says. Dunn also wanted to stay in the Miami area, so she started at Burdines.

It took Dunn three and a half years to get her first buyer's position, in the infant's department. "That was the high point of my career," she remembers, "because I really wanted the job. And I got it."

Dunn, who has her eye on the next step—divisional merchandiser—has seen a lot of changes for women in the business. Sales representatives now tend to be women, while earlier a woman representative was the exception. And there are many more women at the executive level. When asked the most important thing she's discovered along the way, Dunn was philosophical. "Learning how to work and deal with people helped me grow personally," she says. "I was very quick to react when I first started out. Now I accept individuals for who they are."

Glamour and Realities

While the fashion industry is big business and glamorous, there are some hard realities. In New York, for example, most entry-level positions pay between $20,000 and $25,000 a year, a wage that can remain the same for three years before a promotion. In addition, the hours are usually long.[1] Staff members who produce fashions for a runway show, for example, can work up to seventy hours a week for several weeks leading up to the event. And those who are talented and enthusiastic about expressing their artistic skills as designers may have to rein themselves in at their first jobs because their employers probably have already established reputations for a certain look or style. So the new designer has to adapt her or his skills to what the company wants.[2]

What basic skills are essential for a fashion novice and what kinds of jobs are out there? Computer skills are important because today even the smallest companies have a system in place. Also vital is the traditionally valued ability to communicate and work well with people, because fashion is a team effort. Catalogs, which have boomed since the 1970s, have created a fashion niche and so have home shopping networks. Someone has to create clean, accurate, enticing copy that will help a garment sell; someone has to photograph the garments; and someone has to set up the shoots. With the home shopping networks, employees are needed to write scripts, set the stage, organize the show's flow, and select the fashions.[3] Videos are now used by stores to promote a new line, so video production is another possibility. Jobs also exist in fashion-related areas that service the industry, such as advertising, display, forecasting, and publicity.

Have opportunities improved for women who want fashion careers in these times? Marie Essex, chair of the Department of Fashion Design at Parsons School of Design, comments, "I think there are more women moving into design postions who have their names affiliated with small collections."[4] Young women designers are also forming partnerships, and producing clothing lines with labels that reflect the partnerships.

Lenore Benson is the director of archival projects for The Fashion Group International, an association for professional women in fashion and related industries, founded in 1930. The association has over 6,000 members and headquarters in New York City. Benson, who was the Fashion Group's executive director for ten years, says many more women achieved prominence in the design field in the 1940s and 1950s, however she feels that in general, jobs have opened up. "There are more opportunities in business and management postions," she explains. "The industry recognized that women can hold many top jobs. Also young women can now expand into business and legal positions and not just the creative jobs the industry felt were suited for women."[5]

Notes

Chapter 1

1. Ishbel Ross, *Crusades and Crinolines: The Life and Times of Ellen Curtis Demorest and William Jennings Demorest* (New York: Harper & Row, 1963), pp. 20, 22.

2. Ibid., p. 24.

3. Ibid., p. 176.

4. Irene M. Franck and David Brownstone, *Clothiers* (New York, Facts On File, 1987), p. 84.

5. Ibid., p. 82.

6. Ibid., p. 84.

7. Bonnie S. Anderson and Judith Zinsser, *A History of Their Own: Women in Europe from Prehistory to the Present,* vol. I (New York: Harper & Row, 1988), p. 372.

8. Ibid., p. 408.

9. Ibid., pp. 371–372.

10. Franck and Brownstone, p. 131.

11. Anderson and Zinsser, p. 358.

12. Franck and Brownstone, p. 144.

13. Anderson and Zinsser, p. 408.

14. Franck and Brownstone, p. 87.

15. Diana de Marly, *The History of Haute Couture, 1850–1950,* (New York: Holmes and Meier, 1980), p. 11.

16. Franck and Brownstone, p. 108.

17. Elizabeth Wilson, *Adorned in Dreams* (Berkeley: University of California Press, 1985), p. 31.

18. Sara M. Evans, *Born for Liberty: A History of Women in America* (New York: The Free Press, 1989), p. 156.

19. Page Putnam Miller, ed., *Reclaiming the Past: Landmarks of Women's History* (Bloomington: Indiana University Press, 1992), p. 201.

20. Elizabeth Cynthia Barney Buel, *The Tale of the Spinning Wheel* (Cambridge: Cambridge University Press, 1908), p. 37.

21. Robert Breeden, ed., *The Craftsman in America* (Washington, D.C.: National Geographic Society, 1957), p. 96.

22. Buel, p. 39.

23. Evans, p. 51.

24. Buel, p. 51.

25. Mary Beth Norton, *Liberty's Daughters: The Revolutionary Experience of American Women, 1750–1800* (Boston: Little, Brown and Company,), pp. 178–187.

26. Franck and Brownstone, p. 95.

27. Ibid., p. 148.

28. Ibid., p. 38.

29. Breeden, p. 94.

30. Franck and Brownstone, p. 35.

31. Ibid., p. 38.

32. Ibid., p. 40.

33. Ross, p. 8.

34. Franck and Brownstone, p. 40.

Chapter 2

1. Glenna Matthews, *The Rise of Public Woman: Woman's Power and Woman's Place in the United States, 1630–1970* (New York: Oxford University Press, 1992), p. 98.

2. Putnam Miller, p. 203.

3. Steve Dunwell, *The Run of the Mill: A Pictorial Narrative of the Expansion, Dominion, Decline and Enduring Impact of the New England Textile Industry* (Boston: David R. Godine, 1978), p. 33.

4. Buel, p. 36.

5. Breeden, p. 96.

6. Dunwell, p. 32.

7. Ibid., p. 34.

8. Putnam Miller, p. 203.

9. Ibid., p. 20.

10. Dunwell, p. 47.

11. Matthews, p. 97.

12. Franck and Brownstone, p. 77.

13. Putnam Miller, p. 203.

14. Penny Colman, *Strike!* (Brookfield, CT: Millbrook Press, 1995), p. 29.

15. Phillis J. Read and Bernard L. Witlieb, *The Book of Women's Firsts* (New York: Random House, 1992), p. 32.

16. Lynn Sherr and Jurate Kazickas, *Susan B. Anthony Slept Here: A Guide to American Women's Landmarks* (New York: Times Books, 1994), p. 209.

17. Wilson, p. 68.

18. Anne L. Macdonald, *Feminine Ingenuity: Women and Invention in America* (New York: Ballantine Books, 1992), p. xxi.

19. Evans, p. 110.

20. Ibid., p. 109.

21. Putnam Miller, p. 202.

22. Macdonald, p. 5.

23. Matthews, p. 96.

24. Ibid., p. 115.

25. Jessie Carney Smith, ed., *Black Firsts: 2,000 years of Extraordinary Achievement* (Detroit: Visible Ink, 1994), p. 10.

26. Putnam Miller, p. 216.

27. Caroline R. Milbank, *New York Fashion: The Evolution of American Style* (New York: Harry N. Abrams Publishers, 1989), pp. 16, 29.

28. Ibid., p. 19.

29. Read, Witlieb, p. 55.

30. Macdonald, p. 106.

31. Ibid., p. 107.

32 Milbank, p. 22.

33. Franck and Brownstone, p. 97.

34. Milbank, p. 18.

35. Ibid., p. 28.

36. Ibid, p. 38.

37. Ibid., p. 36.

38. Ibid., pp. 22, 25.

39. MacDonald, p. 120.

40. Ibid., p. 65.

41. Ibid., p. 50.

42. Ibid., p. 110.

43. Alan Brinkley, et al., *American History: A Survey,* vol. 2 (New York: McGraw-Hill, 1991), p. 528.

44. Milbank, p. 45.

45. Susan Jonas, ed., *Ellis Island: Echoes from a Nation's Past* (New York: Aperture Inc., 1989), p. 17.

46. William Graebner and Leonard Richards, *The American Record: Images of the Nation's Past* (New York: McGraw-Hill, Inc., 1988), p. 37.

47. Franck and Brownstone, p. 104.

48. Ibid., p. 104.

49. Ibid., p. 105.

50. Brinkley, et. al., p. 528.

51. Ibid., p. 531.

52. Ibid., pp. 531–532.

53. Evans, pp. 157–158.

54. Ibid., p. 58.

55. Matthews, p. 205.

56. Evans, p. 160.

57. Putnam Miller p. 206.

58. Brinkley, et. al., p. 630.

Chapter 3

1. Milbank, pp. 59–60.

2. Ibid., p. 59.

3. Annette Tapert and Diana Edkins, *The Power of Style* (New York: Crown Publishers, Inc., 1994), p. 44.

4. Milbank, p. 59.

5. Valerie Steele, *Paris Fashion: A Cultural History* (New York: Oxford University Press, 1988), pp. 22–24.

6. Ibid., p. 25.

7. Ibid., p. 52.

8. Ibid., p. 229.

9. Milbank, p. 61.

10. Sister Wendy Becket, *The Story of Painting* (New York: Dorling Kindersley, 1994), p. 275.

11. Steele, p. 236.

12. Milbank, p. 62.

13. Putnam Miller, p. 217.

14. Milbank, p. 46.

15. Evans, p. 171–172.

16. Dorothy M. Brown, *Setting a Course: American Women in the 1920s* (Boston: Twayne Publishers, 1987), p. 248.

17. Carney Smith, p. 92.

18. Milbank, p. 46.

19. Bettina Berch, *Radical By Design: The Life and Style of Elizabeth Hawes* (New York: E. P. Dutton, 1988) p. 8.

20. Ibid., p. 14.

21. Ibid., p. 35.

22. Ibid., p. 23.

23. Ibid., p. 21.

24. Ibid., p. 54.

25. Ibid., p. 19.

26. Milbank, p. 98.

27. Berch, p. 44.

28. Ibid., p. 59.

29. Ibid., p. 153.

30. Ibid., p. 45.

31. Ibid., p. 43.

32. Milbank, p. 121.

33. Costume Institute Viewing, September 29, 1994.

34. Milbank, p. 132.

35. Ibid., p. 132.

36. Ibid., pp. 105–106.

37. Ibid., p. 123.

38. Ibid., p. 130.

39. Evans, p. 224

40. Ibid., p. 222.

41. Putnam Miller, p. 218.

42. Doreen Rappaport, *American Women: Their Lives in Their Own Words* (New York: Thomas Y. Crowell, 1990), p. 225.

43. Berch, p. 96.

44. Milbank, p. 136.

45. Ibid., pp. 132–134.

46. Evans, p. 230.

47. Evans, p. 240.

48. Matthews, p. 223.

49. Brinkley, et. al., p. 856.

50. Ibid., p. 868.

51. Ibid., p. 869.

52. Ibid., pp. 879–880.

53. Evans, p. 264.

54. Evans, p. 268.

55. Milbank, p. 211.

Chapter 4

1. Jeannette Jarnow and Miriam Guerreiro, *Inside the Fashion Business*, fifth ed. (New York: Macmillan Publishing Company, 1991), p. 9.

2. Ibid., p. 5.

3. Trip Gabriel, "Hyperbole Takes to the Runway," *New York Times*, Metro Report, October 30, 1994, p. 41; also, Fashion Institute of Technology press release.

4. Jarnow and Guerreiro, p. 421.

5. "Today's Shopping Options," *Consumer Reports*, November, 1994, p. 716.

6. Ibid.

7. Orla Healy, "Clothes Comfort," Now Style, *New York Daily News*, August 25, 1994, p. 57.

8. Gabriel, p. 41; see also Orla Healy, "Skin Is in for '95," *New York Daily News*, October 31, 1994, p. 3.

9. Jarnow and Guerreiro, p. 93.

10. Ibid., p. 100.

11. Ibid., p. 101.

12. Ibid.

13. Ibid., p. 539.

14. Ibid., p. 145.

15. Roslyn Dolber, *Opportunities in Fashion Careers* (Chicago: VGM Career Horizons, 1993), pp. 8, 10.

16. Ibid., p. 11.

17. Dottie Enrico, "Future Fashion Mavens Start Small," *New York Newsday*, October 16, 1994, Money and Careers, p. 7.

18. Jarnow and Guerreiro, p. 144.

19. Dolber, p. 21

20. Jarnow and Guerreiro, p. 144.

21. Healy, Skin Is in for '95, p. 3.

22. Dolber, p. 8.

23. Dolber, p. 21.

24. Dolber, p. 22.

25. Melissa Sones, *Getting into Fashion: A Career Guide* (New York: Ballantine Books, 1984), p. 55.

26. Jarnow and Guerreiro, p. 14.

27. Dolber, p. 19.

28. "Tricks the Stores Use to Sell," *Consumer Reports*, November 1994, p. 717.

29. Ibid.

30. Ibid.

31. Dolber, p. 64.

32. *Lovejoy's College Guide* (Englewood Cliffs: Prentice Hall, 1984).

33. Jarnow and Guerreiro, p. 474.

34. Jarnow and Guerreiro, pp. 64–66.

35. Ibid., p. 66.

36. Sones, p. 99.

37. Dolber, p. 68.

38. Dolber, p. 61.

39. Jarnow and Guerreiro, p. 55.

Chapter 5

1. Personal interview with Carolina Herrera, February 8, 1995.

2. Carrie Donovan, "Social Grace," *New York Times Magazine*, July 10, 1983. p. 34.

3. Earl Blackwell, editor, *Earl Blackwell's Celebrity Register* (Towson, MD: Times Publication Group, 1986).

4. Lynn Barre, "Carolina Herrera in a Class by Herself," *Spotlight*, March, 1991, p. 51.

5. Bernadine Morris, "For Carolina Herrera, Tranquility Amid Success," *New York Times*, January 4, 1994, p. D21.

6. Phone interview with Claire Ortiz, October 26, 1994.

7. Observed beauty shoot with Fashion Director Eve Feurer, January 10, 1995.

8. Personal interviews with Eve Feurer at *New Woman*, January 17 and 20, 1995.

9. Observed Tracy Reese Fashion Show at New York Public Library, November 1, 1994.

10. Orla Healy and Laurice Parkin, "The Vital Statistics," *New York Daily News*, October 30, 1994, p. 22.

11. Personal interview with Tracy Reese, November 17, 1994.

12. Telephone interview with Tracy Reese, January 12, 1994.

13. Comment from Marie Essex, associate chairperson of fashion design, Parsons School of Design.

14. Personal interview on November 17, 1994; telephone interview January 19, 1995.

15. Telephone interview with Sharon Covey, November 15, 1994.

16. Telephone interview with Jackie Corso, November 15, 1994.

17. Personal interviews with Patricia Kaneb, November 25 and December 12, 1994.

18. Susan Diesenhouse, "Can She Take Priscilla's Place at the Altar," *New York Times*, October 9, 1994.

19. Personal interviews with Maryann Puglisi, February 1 and March 3, 1995.

20. Personal interviews with Dennita Sewell, January 23 and 30, 1995.

21. Janet Ozzard, "Forever Viv," *Women's Wear Daily*, September 13, 1994.

22. Personal interview with Zelda Wynn, May 30, 1996.

23. Telephone interview with Arthur Mitchell, June 4, 1996.

24. Telephone interview with Andrea Ross, May 30, 1996.

25. Telephone interview with Lydia Caffery, December 22, 1994.

26. Interview with Bill Daddy, January 25, 1995.

27. Personal interview with Yvette Fry, April 27, 1995.

28. Personal interview with Yvette Fry, May 2, 1995.

29. Telephone interview with Laura Dunn, May 4, 1995.

30. Telephone interview with Laura Dunn, May 8, 1995.

Chapter 6

1. Enrico, p. 7.

2. Ibid.

3. Ibid.

4. Telephone interview with Marie Essex, June 19, 1996

5. Telephone interview with Lenore Benson, June 19, 1996.

Further Reading

Berch, Bettina. *Radical by Design: The Life and Style of Elizabeth Hawes, Fashion Designer, Union Organizer, Best-Selling Author.* New York: E. P. Dutton, 1988.

Dorner, Jane. *The Changing Shape of Fashion Through the Years.* London: Octopus Press, 1974.

Fashions of a Decade. 8 vols. New York: Facts On File, 1990–1992.

Macdonald, Anne L. *Feminine Ingenuity: Women and Invention in America.* New York: Balantine Books, 1992.

Milbank, Caroline R. *New York Fashion: The Evolution of Style.* New York: Harry N. Abrams, 1989.

Walz, Barbara, and Bernadine Morris. *The Fashion Makers: An Inside Look at America's Leading Designers.* New York: Random House, 1978.

Schurnberger, Lynn. *Let There Be Clothes: 40,000 Years of Fashion.* New York: Workman Publishing, 1991.

Index

Numbers in *italics* indicate illustrations.

About the Author

Linda Leuzzi is a journalist and syndicated feature writer whose articles have appeared in *Newsday, Family Circle, Ladies Home Journal, New Woman,* and other periodicals. She is the author of several books on aspects of American history, and her work was included in *Reading the Environment,* an environmental text for college students.

Ms. Leuzzi was formerly a public relations manager for Avon Products and an associate editor at King Features Syndicate. She is a member of the Newswomen's Club of New York and the American Association of Journalists and Authors. She earned a B.S. in journalism at St. John's University and she lives in Queens, New York.